DATE

TALK,

DINNER

TALK,

PILLOW

TALK

DATE TALK, DINNER TALK, PILLOW TALK

WHAT MEN THINK ABOUT WHAT YOU SAY

KEN CARLTON

AVON BOOKS  NEW YORK

AVON BOOKS, INC.
1350 Avenue of the Americas
New York, New York 10019

Copyright © 1998 by Ken Carlton
Published by arrangement with the author
Visit our website at **http://www.AvonBooks.com**
ISBN: 0-380-79802-6

Library of Congress Cataloging in Publication Data:

Date talk, dinner talk, pillow talk : what men think about what you
    say / [collected by] Ken Carlton.
        p.   cm.
        1. Interpersonal communication—United States.   2. Man-woman
    relationships—United States.   3. Conversation analysis—United
    States.   I. Carlton, Ken.
    BF637.C45D345   1998   98-4764
    306.73—dc21   CIP

First Avon Books Trade Printing: July 1998

AVON TRADEMARK REG. U.S. PAT. OFF. AND IN OTHER COUNTRIES, MARCA REGISTRADA, HECHO
EN U.S.A.

Printed in the U.S.A.

OPM   10 9 8 7 6 5 4 3 2 1

Contents

DATE
TALK,
DINNER
TALK,
PILLOW
TALK

Introduction

The greatest conversation I've ever had with a woman consisted mainly of silence. We sat on a mountaintop in Vermont and watched the sun go down for about half an hour. Then we had a five-word dialogue. I asked, "Will you marry me?" And happily, fortunately, she replied, "Yes."

Of course it took me a dozen years of dating and some of the most inane conversations in history to get to that point. But frankly, all those years of idle banter taught me a thing or two about listening and illustrated a lot of the basic differences between women and men.

So why a book on dating dialogues? Because other than sex, the number one topic men talk about *behind* women's backs are the incredible things they say on dates. The hysterical and frustrating and sexy and touching and aggravating and utterly endearing things you talk about to win our attention and capture our hearts.

This book is a collection of these conversations. They have been gathered and retold by dozens of men and women sharing the intimate details of dialogues they've had and conversations they wish they hadn't had. Naturally, the names and certain details have been changed, but the sentiments are as real as the people who lived them.

If relationships were only about desire, courtship, and

sex, every single person would be married, and the divorce rate would be zero. However, the reality is that we all talk ourselves blue in the face looking for the right relationship—the one that becomes a lifelong dialgue. This book is a random sampling of the things people talk about on dates—words that kill, and conversations that lead to the kind of understanding that makes the best couples seem as if they've known each other forever.

Ken Carlton
Rockport, Massachusetts

Chapter 1
THE ASKING

The Classic Bar Pickup

The setup:

The Chicago Bulls are in the finals (again) and a big crowd of Yuppie-types are gathered after work to watch Game 1 in a friendly, neighborhood pub. A half dozen guys and girls sort of know each other from frequenting this bar, so conversation with a near stranger is not exactly unwarranted.

TOM
(Joking to an attractive woman)
Howdy! Come here often?

He winks at her suggestively.

WOMAN
(Also joking—exaggerated)
Absolutely! All the time. My love life is in

such desperate straits I hang out at bars waiting for scintillating pickup lines like that.

TOM

Ouch! Well, you know, the only reason I'm watching the game here is because I gave my season tickets to my dad and brother.

WOMAN

Is this the part where I think you're a superswell guy because of your extraordinary sense of sacrifice?

TOM

No. It's the part where you were *supposed* to say, "Ohhh, you have season tickets?"

WOMAN
(Playing along)
Okay. "Wow! You have season tickets?"

TOM

Nope. Just joking. I don't even have a good view of the TV!

WOMAN

Well maybe you'll do better tomorrow night, because me and my girlfriends won't be here.

TOM

Oh no. Why not?

WOMAN

Because we'll be at the game . . . with *my* season tickets!

>   TOM
>   (Impressed)
>   You have season tickets?

>   WOMAN
>   Wouldn't you like to know!
>   (Reaches into her purse and
>   hands Tom her business card)
>   Call me. Find out!

She walks away to rejoin her girlfriends.

Tom's Take:

Bingo! Winner. Men love a good sense of humor, not to
mention a woman who can dish it as well as she takes it.
Tom used the ol' lounge-lizard-imitation pickup routine,
and this woman turned it upside down right on his head.
Two minutes at a bar and he has her card and they have
history. A definite phoner tomorrow!

Cream with that Coffee?

The setup:

Cory hangs out at the local designer coffee shop in his
neighborhood where he frequently sees an attractive
woman, Marta. They've made eye contact dozens of times,
exchanged hellos, even read the paper side by side on
a weekend. Finally, the day comes when the ice must
be broken.

CORY
(Paper under his arm)
So, we meet again.

MARTA
(Looks up from her paper)
Oh. Hey, how are you?

CORY
Glad it's the weekend.

MARTA
That makes two of us. . . . Say, my name's
Marta.

CORY
Cory. Nice to meet you. Or at least meet you
formally.

MARTA
Yeah, it's funny, isn't it? You see someone
every day for a year and never know their
name. Until now—

CORY
No kidding. So, ummm, you obviously live
around here.

MARTA
Just up the block. At Eighteenth Street. What
about you?

CORY
One down. Seventeenth Street.

MARTA
No kidding. Great neighborhood, isn't it?

CORY

I've lived here five years. Love it. Say, can you pass the sugar please?

MARTA
(Tsk tsking)

You shouldn't use that stuff. It'll put you in an early grave.

CORY

I'll take my chances. So, do you eat out around here a lot?

MARTA

I like to cook. I don't go out to dinner too much.

CORY

Well maybe we should grab a bite one night. You like Chinese?

MARTA

Are you kidding? All that grease, and MSG? No way.

CORY
(Furrowing his eyebrows)

I know a great Mexican place on Twenty-third Street.

MARTA

Cheese clogs your arteries. Might as well have open heart surgery before dinner.

CORY

How about sushi?

MARTA
Sorry. I'm a vegetarian. Much better for your lower G.I.

CORY
(Gets up with his coffee)
Well, uhhhh, Marta. Swell meeting you.

MARTA
Yeah. Great meeting you, too. Dinner sometime sounds nice. Maybe I'll cook for you?

Cory's Take:

Not likely. Marta has given out way too much information way too quickly. Dating is supposed to be fun, exciting, and adventurous. When we're fantasizing about undressing you with our eyes over a nice juicy steak and red wine, the last thing we want to hear about is clogged arteries. Cory might have been interested at first, but Marta has laid out such a strong line about her food requirements that Cory has to be wincing. Try to keep the unusual dietary needs to a minimum in a first-date situation. When a man asks you out he is looking for a spark, not a health warning from his mother.

The Friendly Skies

The setup:

Somewhere over New Jersey, the Friday night shuttle, New York City to Washington, D.C. As usual, this flight is jammed to the gills. There are no seating assignments and Mike, a well-dressed businessman has seated himself next to Veronica, an equally well-dressed businesswoman. Mike, who fell asleep twelve seconds after takeoff has just woken up.

MIKE
(Looking confused, to his seatmate)
Oh man, what a nap! I'm sorry. Did I snore?

VERONICA
(Looks up from her book)
No, nothing serious. You muttered a couple of things about a prison shower. I didn't pay attention.

MIKE
(Smiling)
Yeah well—that was a long time ago.

VERONICA
(Smiles back)
Look, it's none of my business, but you might want to wipe that strand of drool off your chin. It's about to hit your collar.

Mike slaps his hand to his face in horror.

VERONICA
(Goes back to her book)
Just kidding . . .

The flight attendant, making her rounds, stops at their row.

MIKE
I'll have a Coke. And my companion here—

VERONICA

Coke is fine.

MIKE

(To the flight attendant)
My round. Please!

Naturally, the drinks are free.

VERONICA

You're too kind.

MIKE

Any time. . . . So, watcha doing in
Washington?

VERONICA

Spending the weekend with my friend Barry.
I think we're going to dinner in Georgetown
tonight. Then dancing. Then who knows
what?

MIKE

Sounds promising. Lucky guy!

VERONICA

Lucky girl. She's my best friend from college.

MIKE

Whoops!

VERONICA

And you?

MIKE

Going home. Just in New York for business.

VERONICA
You live in Washington?

MIKE
Georgetown.

VERONICA
Nice. I love Georgetown.

MIKE
You go there often?

VERONICA
(Smiling at him)
As often I as get invited. . . .

Mike's Take:

The airline pickup is one of the trickiest moves in the game for a guy. It's such an obvious (and confining) spot that you can either strike up a new friendship or make a complete imbecile of yourself. Veronica put out all the right signals to catch Mike's attention—and she wasn't pathetic or overbearing as a seatmate. Based on that fun five-minute conversation, she opened the door for Mike to offer a business card or perhaps even suggest a meeting at a local Georgetown bar. Safe, non-threatening, and with a thousand easy outs if neither wanted to pursue it. Veronica played her cards perfectly and an interested man would pick up those signals in a heartbeat.

Risky Business

The setup:

Pauline's worked together for over a year with Tom, a guy who pushes all the right buttons for her. They both flirt constantly. She likes his smile, his easygoing manner, and he's definitely *not* wearing a wedding band. Only problem? He's never asked her out. They run into each other in the office kitchen.

> PAULINE
> You were really funny in the staff meeting this morning.

> TOM
> Oh come on. You know everyone was dying to tell Poindexter that the whole project is a zero.

> PAULINE
> Yeah, maybe. But not everyone has the nerve.

> TOM
> Oh well. I used to host a radio show in college. I guess I'm used to offering loud opinions to anyone who will listen.

> PAULINE
> You were a deejay?

> TOM
> Many moons ago.

> PAULINE
> Get out. Me too. What format music?

TOM
I did this hip-hop thing before anyone knew
what hip-hop was.

PAULINE
That's so funny. Before they got big I inter-
viewed the Fugees for the Syracuse radio
station.

TOM
Wow. That's very cool. I love the Fugees.

Pauline offers Tom the crusty coffee creamer jar as they
chat.

PAULINE
Say. Do you know that club, Houston's, down
on Fourth Street?

TOM
Can't say I do.

PAULINE
They do a hip-hop evening on Tuesdays. Great
burgers, too. You want to check it out
sometime?

TOM
Yeah. Sure. Why not. That sounds like a lot of
fun.

PAULINE
I'll see what's on next week and e-mail you?

TOM
Cool. I'm game. . . .

Tom's Take:

Did he just get asked out on a date? Sounds like it, but oh how subtle the overtones. The perfect opening gambit. Pauline obviously knows Tom well enough to be casual. Their informal office chat uncovered a mutual interest. And most important, she left a dozen doors open with her informal invite. Tom could just say no. He could suggest they ask a few more people to join them. Or he could jump on the invite and suggest they make it an evening, dinner and the lot. Great maneuvering and opening lines on Pauline's part. Risk-free, yet inviting. Plus, it leaves Tom with that intriguing thought: "Say, does she like me?"

The Film Critic

The setup:

It's Saturday night and Maureen and her roommate Cindy are browsing Tom Cruise movies at the local video store. It's so obvious Maureen does not have a date that she might as well stamp "Loser" on her forehead. Of course this doesn't bother her a lick because there's nothing wrong with a night home with a girlfriend. That is, until an interesting-looking young man literally stumbles over her in the action adventure aisle—and he is alone, with the same "Loser" stamp written all over *his* forehead.

GREG
Oh. Excuse me.

MAUREEN
Excuse *me*. I wasn't looking.

They both glance at one another's video selections.

> GREG
> *Top Gun* . . . good flick.

> MAUREEN
> I've seen it already. I was just, we were just—
> you know, renting it for fun.

> GREG
> The Tom Cruise thing. I understand.

> MAUREEN
> What's that you've got?

> GREG
> Ummm—a small foreign film. It's nothing. *Un
> Coeur en Hiver?*

> MAUREEN
> *A Heart in Winter.* I love Emmanuelle Beart. I
> think she's so beautiful. Did you see that one
> where she posed nude for some painter for
> like the whole movie?

> GREG
> No. But maybe I better go look for it.

> MAUREEN
> (Laughing)
> An Emmanuel Beart double feature. Sounds
> like a hot date to me!

Maureen's friend Cindy joins them.

> CINDY
> Hey, c'mon. I'm starving. Let's order up a

pizza—Ooops. Sorry. I didn't mean to
interrupt.

GREG

Not at all. Your friend was just recommending
a little French perversion for my Saturday
night.

CINDY
(Sensing a "love connection")
Yeah well, Maureen goes for that artsy-fartsy
thing. I'm more of a Keanu/Tom kind of person. You know?

GREG

Really? I go more for the mind-numbing mean-
ing-of-life kind of movies. Preferably de-
pressing as hell!

CINDY
(Rolling her eyes)
Oh boy. You guys are made for each other.
Maybe I'll just get a big fat pepperoni pizza
and go suffer through *Top Gun* and you guys
can order up some escargot or something and
have a "cinema" party.

MAUREEN
(Sufficiently embarrassed)
Yes, Miss Virginia-Woolf-on-her-nightstand.
Time to take you home before you humiliate
me any more.

CINDY
(To Greg)
That's what friends are for, right? I'm Cindy.
This is Maureen. Vassar '94. English major.
Working for her masters in teaching at Colum-

bia. Likes the beach and skiing. Oh, and she's a vegetarian, but only after you get to know her.

GREG
(Shakes Maureen's hand, a bit shy now)
I'm Greg. Hi. Umm, I guess I better be going.

MAUREEN
Yeah. Nice meeting you. Sorry about my roommate—

CINDY
(Tugging Maureen along)
C'mon, honey. We've got a hot date with Mister Cruise and the boys. . . .
(To Greg)
She usually rents here a couple of times a week. Around seven. Oh, and she loves classical music. . . . Bye!

The girls make their way to the front of the store, leaving a bemused Greg behind.

Greg's Take:

He will be renting in this store every weekday around seven for the next year in the hopes of bumping into Maureen again. Chemistry is a funny thing. It can be oozing between two people, but single humans are shy by nature—and we all spend countless days and nights wondering why we didn't make the move when the "moment" occurred. In this case, thank goodness for the talkative roommate. Obviously Greg and Maureen didn't object to her meddling. And without Cindy's intervention, it was unlikely Greg and Maureen would have gotten anywhere near this much information on each other—and the chance to meet again.

INSIDER'S TIP: Men are like dogs. Once they've got the scent, they will definitely come back many times in search of the owner. If you have a successful chance encounter— at a video store, the market, the bank—retrace your tracks several times over. There's a fine chance the man you met will be sniffing around hoping for that marvelous "coincidence" of meeting again so he can have the excuse to ask you out.

The Office Cubicle Lurker

The setup:

It's a Wednesday morning and Lucy's deeply engaged in a really important business call—with her best girlfriend! She notices a guy from accounting whom she vaguely knows, hanging out by her cubicle. He seems to want something. She can tell because he's reading everything in sight (including fire marshal instructions on the wall), and he hasn't budged from her field of vision in the past ten minutes.

> LUCY
> (On the phone)
> Look, I've got to run.
> (Whispered)
> I'll call you back in a sec.

Lucy hangs up the phone and pretends to go back to work. This guy, Bill, continues to lurk.

LUCY
(Finally, to Bill)
Can I help you with something?

BILL
(Utterly surprised)
Ughhh, me?

LUCY
Well yeah. I noticed you hanging out.

BILL
(Blushing)
Oh. Umm, I was sort of waiting to talk to Jane
Smith about her expense report—
(He points to a closed door)
—I'm, uhhh, Bill. In accounting?

LUCY
Yeah. I know who you are. Jane's in Gdansk
for a week. Her grandmother died.

Lucy goes back to work. Bill moves in closer. It's apparent
his interest in Jane was secondary.

BILL
Oh. That's too bad. . . . Aren't you Lucy
Bunn?

LUCY
Yeah?

BILL
I'm Bill Jones. I get your expense reports.
You're very good.

LUCY
(Utterly suspicious)
At what!

BILL
Your reports. They're always so—organized.
I'm sure you're a very organized person.

LUCY
I suppose so.

BILL
You'd be amazed at the stuff people turn in.
You know, like scribbled on toilet paper and
the backs of sandwich bags. I once had a guy
accidentally give me his expenses on the back
of a cocktail napkin with the name of some
girl he met in Pittsburgh.

LUCY
You don't say?

BILL
No, I'm serious. You learn some wild stuff
about people when you see the things they
turn in for expenses. . . .

LUCY
I'm sure. Anyway, I've got like a ton of stuff
to do so if you'll excuse me—

BILL
(Disappointed)
Oh. Sorry to bug you. See you around?

LUCY
I'll tell Jane you stopped by. When she gets
backs from Gdansk.

BILL
(Finally gives up)
Right. When she gets back from Gdansk . . .

Lucy picks up the phone to call her friend back. Bill skulks away.

Bill's Take:

He'll probably find a new job before he ever has to wander into this corner of the office again. Men are not born lurkers. Bill obviously wanted to find some spark with Lucy and she either found him utterly unappealing or she missed the signals. If you see a man looking bored anywhere near your desk, he is waiting to find an excuse to talk to you. Any excuse! It is because there is something about you that he finds attractive. Of course there is no law that says you have to make conversation with him. But don't for a second be fooled by the fumbling excuse he makes for hanging out. He is laying out chum and hoping you bite.

Safety in Numbers

The setup:

Paul works out at the same health club on the same days almost always at the exact same time. He even works out in the same order—treadmill, Nautilus, free weights—for one hour three times a week. So it's no big surprise that he has actually come to know Missy, a woman from his neighborhood, by face if not by name. They occasionally chat, laugh, and grunt at each other but have never formally introduced themselves in the six months they've been on the same workout schedule.

                    PAUL
        (Getting off the treadmill, drenched)
    Hey. How ya doing?

                    MISSY
        (Just getting on the treadmill)
    Good. How about you?

                    PAUL
    I'm tired today. Jet-lagged. That run nearly killed me.

                    MISSY
    Really? Where were you?

                    PAUL
    London for a couple of days. No biggie, but I never adjust to the time change on short trips to Europe.

                    MISSY
    Do you go to Europe a lot?

                    PAUL
    Once every couple of months.

                    MISSY
    That sounds nice. What do you do?

                    PAUL
    Nothing very interesting. I'm a banker.

                    MISSY
    Europe every couple of months doesn't sound so bad.

PAUL

I guess I can't complain. How about you. You ever get out of town?

MISSY

I went to Cleveland last month!

PAUL

Very nice. What's in Cleveland?

MISSY

A big lake . . . oh, and a bunch of would-be sci-fi authors.

PAUL

Really. Are you a writer?

MISSY

Editor. I've currently got our science-fiction line. I get to speak to some of America's biggest nuts. You'd be amazed how many people have a one-on-one relationship with aliens.

PAUL

Sounds fun . . .

Missy ups the pace on the treadmill. Paul has that hungry look of a guy who wants to talk more, but he doesn't want to interfere with her workout. Missy seems interested, too.

PAUL (Cont'd)

Well, I'll let you sweat.

MISSY

Thanks. . . . Say, ummm—uhhh, I don't even know your name—

PAUL
Paul! And I know what you mean. We see
each other three times a week and—

MISSY
(Picks up on the moment)
Missy! I live over on Thirtieth.

PAUL
Great! I'm in the Windsor on Thirty-
second. . . . Anyway—

MISSY
Say, uhhh, Paul? Do you play softball?

PAUL
Used to. Been a long time.

MISSY
Well, if you're not doing anything this weekend, me and three girlfriends are having a big
party at the park. We're inviting about a gazil-
lion different people.

PAUL
No kidding.

MISSY
Yeah. You know, a small intimate gathering of
everyone we've ever known?

PAUL
Sounds great.

MISSY
So if you wanted to come on by and bring a
couple dozen of your best friends, that might

be sort of fun. Over by the fields on 110th Street. Anytime from noon on.

PAUL
I might just do that.

MISSY
I'll be looking for you. . . .

Paul's Take:

Opportunity is knocking loudly at the door and you can bet he's going to follow up this generous invite from Missy. How does a girl ask a guy out? Just offer softball, beer, and friends in a casual setting and men will flock like moths to flame. In this particular case, since Missy and Paul have been eyeballing each other for six months at the club anyway, this is a chance to hang out together casually with no pressure. Should their day in the park turn out to be a winner, then a real date could come out of it. Kudos to Missy for taking the lead.

A Good Tip

The setup:

Emily waits tables at a family pizza house in a college town. She is serving a large group of people all about her age—couples and a few unattached guys and girls. One guy, Phil, seems to be paying special attention to her.

EMILY
(Checking their table)
You guys doing okay?

PHIL

I think we're set. You might bring a garden
hose to spray off Big Bill, though. He's scary
around a large pie.

BIG BILL
(With a mouthful)
Veddy fu-u-uny. Hey, pass the Parmesan.

EMILY
(Laughing at him)
I'll bring extra napkins.

She returns with a fistful a moment later.

EMILY

Let me know if you need anything else.

PHIL

Well, actually, I could use, ummm, well maybe
another Coke?

EMILY
(Staring at his full glass)
You haven't touched that one!

PHIL

Good point. Okay. How about three more
large pies? Everything on them?

EMILY

You expecting a busload any minute?

PHIL

No. But I'd be happy to come help you make
them just to get away from these—
(Refers to his friends)
—meatballs!

EMILY
They seem pretty harmless.

PHIL
That's because you don't know them.

EMILY
Well I've only been here three weeks. Give me
a chance.

PHIL
I thought you looked new. You're—starting
school here next week?

EMILY
Good guess.

PHIL
Pure luck.

PHIL'S FRIEND
Watch him. He's a hound dog.

PHIL
You'll forgive my friends. It's way past their
feeding time.

EMILY
I've been a waitress before. I can handle it.

PHIL
They're harmless once they've been fed and
bathed.

EMILY
No doubt. And you?

PHIL
My day to watch them.

EMILY
What a kind soul!

PHIL
It's dirty work, but someone's got to do it.

EMILY
Look, I'd love to stay and chat, but I better
watch my other tables.

PHIL
Will you bring me the check when it's ready?

EMILY
Okay.

PHIL
I want to be sure and overtip you
dramatically.

EMILY
(Onto his game)
No need. . . . Why don't you just hang out 'til
I'm off and find out if I'm interested?

PHIL
(Intrigued)
Really? When are you off?

EMILY
(Looks at her watch)
Seven more hours . . .

She winks at him good-naturedly and walks away.

Phil's Take:

He'll be there. This may be the corniest pickup routine in the world, but that's the way it works in highly public places. Guys won't risk actually asking you out in front of their friends, but they will drop every line in the book hoping to capture your interest. All Emily need do is write her name and a little smiley face on the check and she can stake her week's salary that Phil *will* be waiting to ask her out at quitting time.

CAREER ADVICE: Women who work at restaurants and in retail are in prime jobs for meeting men. Don't ask why, but it's probably our version of being attracted to someone "in uniform." Waitresses, salesclerks, Gap employees—they all just turn us on and we'll do cartwheels to get their attention, or better yet, phone number!

Work or Pleasure?

The setup:

Don is a sales executive for a West Coast technology company. He attends about a dozen sales meetings a year with a major client in New York and has a joking, friendly relationship with Carla—a manager at the company he visits. At the end of a well-attended meeting, he finds himself chatting alone with Carla by the conference room.

> DON
> Well, that meeting seemed to go well.

> CARLA
> I think everyone's happy with the product.

You've really done a terrific job on the support
end.

DON
(Modestly)
Thanks, but I can hardly take sole credit.
We've got quite a team working on these pre-
sentations back in California.

CARLA
I'm sure they're terrific, but without your pol-
ish it wouldn't be half as impressive.

DON
Well gosh, you know how to make a guy
blush.

CARLA
(Looks at him closely)
You really are blushing, aren't you? I thought
that was just your permanent California tan.

DON
One would occasionally have to see the outdoors to get a tan. The past few months I've
been living in airplanes and boardrooms.

CARLA
On the road all the time?

DON
Constantly.

CARLA
Do you ever get a chance to see the towns you
visit?

DON

I wish. I mean I come to New York a dozen times a year and I couldn't name one restaurant more than a block from my hotel.

CARLA

Well that's no good, is it.

DON

Yes, the lonely life on the road. . . . Anyway, I guess I should get back to my hotel and check my e-mail.

CARLA
(Looking at her watch)
Gosh, the day's almost over, isn't it?

DON

Just flew by. So, I'll be seeing you next trip?

CARLA

Absolutely. . . . Say, are you flying out this evening?

DON

Nope. First thing tomorrow morning.

CARLA

Forgive me for being forward, but if you don't have any big plans tonight, would you like to get out of your hotel room for a change of scenery?

DON

Oh, I wouldn't want to be an imposition. You folks have already taken wonderful care of me today.

CARLA
Well what if the invite was off company time?

DON
You mean, as in—recreation?

CARLA
Actually in New York we call it "fun." But if you prefer, we can just call it dinner.

DON
That's awfully nice of you, but you don't have to do that—

CARLA
Do you like pasta?

DON
Of course.

CARLA
Did you bring a pair of jeans?

DON
Sure did.

CARLA
Well, if I'm not imposing on you, it would be my pleasure to take you out to the best little Italian joint in the Village. We don't have to mention a word of business.

DON
That's an awfully appealing offer.

CARLA
Does that mean you're in?

Don's Take:

Absolutely! How could a guy turn down a great invitation like that. In this day and age of sexual harassment, work-related invites have to be handled delicately. No one wants to be perceived as crossing the line. In Carla's case, she was very clear in her intentions. This is for fun, not work. If Don was not interested, he could decline without seeming rude or unprofessional. And if he accepts, they both know exactly what the score is and can behave accordingly.

Chapter 2
THE DATES
MEN REMEMBER

A Business Affair

The setup:

Tom is out with Lindsay, an investment banker he met at a cocktail party. It is a standard, after-work, weeknight, dinner date. The main course has just been served and Tom is hunting for some spark to light up what has been a less-than-magical evening.

> TOM
> (Cutting into his osso bucco)
> . . . Anyway, Lindsay, so much for work.
> What do you like to do when you hang out?
> You know, weekends, vacations, stuff like
> that?

> LINDSAY
> Vacations? Ha! Is that when you go away *with-out* your laptop and cell phone?

TOM

Yeah, last I heard. . . . Me and a buddy went sailing last fall down on the Chesapeake. Do you sail?

LINDSAY

Nahh. I dated a guy who did, but I didn't really get it. I mean you do all this work just to get from Point A to Point B. Why not just drive?

TOM
(A bit deflated)

Oh. I guess you're not much into sailing. What *do* you like to do?

LINDSAY

Well, if I ever found any free time, I'd like to sleep for about three years.

TOM
(Laughing)

And after you've caught up on your sleep?

LINDSAY

I really haven't thought about it much lately.

TOM
(Really trying here)

There must be something. You know, cooking, reading, macramé?

LINDSAY

I used to ski. That was a long time ago. Before I got this job.

TOM

I love skiing. Haven't been all season.

(Lights up)
Hey, it's supposed to snow like the dickens Friday night. Maybe we should book a car and head for the hills Saturday? You know, just on a lark? Kinda crazy—

LINDSAY
I don't think so. I've got a presentation I have to work on all weekend. It's for a really big client!

Tom nods and refocuses his attention on his osso bucco.

Tom's Take:

Lindsay may be the next Donald Trump, but who wants to date a workaholic. Tom tried to shift the conversation in every positive way he knew, without being too nosy. He asked Lindsay on three separate occasions what she did for fun and three times she somehow swung the conversation back to work. Either Lindsay is way too obsessed with her job, or perhaps she just doesn't care for Tom. Either way, it would seem to any guy that Tom has made the ol' college try. And you know how guys think in general? Three strikes and "yer outta there!"

FREE ADVICE: Talking about nothing but work on a first date is extraordinarily un-sexy. And it's a supercommon complaint amongst males. Impress us with your myriad skills and talents, but don't forget to share a few personal anecdotes as well. If we wanted to talk about work, we would have stayed at the office.

A Blind Date with Good Vision

The setup:

Martin is out on a blind date with Sylvia, to whom he was introduced by a mutual friend, Katherine. Martin and Sylvia live in a major city and have met for drinks after work, still in their suits from the office. They've only been together for about twenty minutes (one beer), but as these things go, they seem to be getting along pretty well.

> MARTIN
> So was *anything* Katherine told you about me true?

> SYLVIA
> Oh, a detail or two. I'd say you pretty much fit your description. What about me?

> MARTIN
> Based on our first thirty minutes together? I'd say I owe our mutual friend a thank-you.

> SYLVIA
> That's very nice of you. . . .

Sylvia blushes appropriately, enjoying the compliment.

> MARTIN
> Say, do you think we've cleared the "first drink we-can-stand-each-other" phase yet?

> SYLVIA
> I'm feeling pretty good about that.

MARTIN
Good. Me too. Can I ask you out on a second
date now?

SYLVIA
(A little confused)
Yeah sure, I guess so.

MARTIN
(With great aplomb)
Would you like to continue these cocktails
over dinner tonight?

SYLVIA
The pleasure would be mine. . . .

Martin and Sylvia exit the crowded bar heading for
greener pastures, when Sylvia takes his arm.

SYLVIA
Well now that we're so comfortable together,
can I ask *you* something personal?

MARTIN
Sure!

SYLVIA
I was thinking, how would you feel if we both
got out of our clothes—
          (Martin raises his eyebrows)
—our *work*clothes, and into something more
casual.

MARTIN
You mean like jeans—

SYLVIA
—and a T-shirt.

MARTIN

So Chez Couchon dans les Bois is out for dinner tonight?

SYLVIA

A little fancy. I was thinking more along the lines of, say, Pomeroy's Brew and Pub?

MARTIN

Burgers and beer.

SYLVIA

I'll drink red wine if you've still got French on the brain.

MARTIN

And I'll have french fries!

SYLVIA

Ouch!

MARTIN
(Feigning hurt)

Didn't Katherine tell you about my sense of humor?

SYLVIA

Yes. But I told her I'd go out with you anyway!

MARTIN
(As they walk along)

Very funny. . . . So we're changing out of our suits first?

SYLVIA

My place or yours???

She winks at him, and they set off walking.

Martin's Take:

Considering the success rate of blind dating, Martin is already dancing in the street, and he's only known Sylvia for thirty minutes. What did she do right? A healthy dose of honesty tempered with an infectious good mood. Clearly their conversation was moving along at a brisk clip, so when Martin suggested dinner, she was in for the long haul. The capper was her suggestion to change into something more comfortable. That says to a guy, "Hey, I like you. You're easy to hang with." And guys love that. "Hanging out" is our national pastime, and men spend countless hours wondering why it's so hard to be friends with a woman. So when you take the lead on making a date a little more fun (translation: a little less uptight), that's a great message to send a guy with whom you feel right at home.

A Little Whine with Dinner?

The setup:

Mitchell and Robin are out at a very expensive oh-so-chic restaurant on a first date. They were set up by their respective mothers, who know one another vaguely from the country club. Robin is a sales representative for a top-end designer. Mitchell trades pork and cattle futures on the commodities market and makes beaucoup bucks. They are seated at a less-than-desirable table much too close to the kitchen, and their appetizer dishes are just being cleared.

ROBIN
I told you this table would be too noisy.

MITCHELL
Hey c'mon. I was lucky to get a reservation.
You told me this was where you wanted to
come for dinner. You said you always come
here.

ROBIN
(Under her breath)
Yeah, usually at a better table.

MITCHELL
(Did not hear her)
Hunghh? I guess it is kind of noisy. Oh
well . . . how was your appetizer?

ROBIN
Average.

MITCHELL
I thought you said this place was supposed to
be terrific.

ROBIN
I'm used to getting a little more special
attention.

MITCHELL
(Under his breath)
So you're sleeping with the chef?

ROBIN
(Missed that remark)
Excuse me?

MITCHELL
I said I'm sure the main course will be better.
Anyway, you were telling me you get to travel
a lot on your job?

ROBIN
I get to Rome. Milan. Paris. Nothing special.

MITCHELL
Paris, boy. That sounds nice.

ROBIN
Yeah it's okay. I was there the other day.

MITCHELL
Really? Just for the day? Did you Concorde
over?

ROBIN
(Very nonchalant)
Of course.

MITCHELL
God that must be cool.

ROBIN
The seats are too small.

MITCHELL
The seats are too small?

ROBIN
And the food is way overrated.

MITCHELL
As compared to what?

ROBIN
(Getting miffed)
Excuse me?

MITCHELL
Gosh, I'm sorry. Just all this noise back
here . . .

A waiter comes over and delicately serves their dinner.

MITCHELL
Well, there you go. Hopefully *this* food lives
up to the billing.

Robin checks out the plate suspiciously.

ROBIN
(To the waiter)
Excuse me. Is Michel in the kitchen tonight?

WAITER
But of course.

ROBIN
I'd like to see him.

The waiter eyeballs their pathetic table in the north forty
of the restaurant.

WAITER
I'm afraid he is very busy tonight, madame.

MITCHELL
Is something wrong, Robin?

ROBIN
(Glares at both of them)
These vegetables are oversteamed! Take them
back.

The waiter rolls his eyebrows, but takes her plate. A tray
crashes in the kitchen. Mitchell looks at his watch. . . .

Mitchell's Take:

"Help, get me out of here!" There are probably guys who
get a kick out of trendy women who go to all the right
places. However, these are generally guys who are intimate friends with Mick Jagger, Bobby De Niro, and Jack
Nicholson. It's hard enough going out with a woman
who expects to be catered to hand and foot. It's even
worse when she alludes to the fact that her previous
dates had better connections or took her to better places.
If Mitchell survives this dinner without clubbing Robin
with a limp asparagus spear, it will be a miracle. First
dates are supposed to be fun. No man alive can guaran-
tee perfection, and most won't waste a lot of second
dates trying!

FIRST DATE WARNING: There are certain behaviors that
always prompt the kind of locker-room talk most women
would dread (if they only knew). Being a whiner, com-
plainer, or snob is one of those universal male dislikes.
Translation: lighten up on a first date. If we can't laugh
together with you, we're probably not going to get very
far.

Remind Me to Have a Chat with Mom

The setup:

Risa is a quiet, bookish, single woman in her mid-twenties, who, if the truth be known, is not all that concerned that her dating life has been flagging of late. However, her mother certainly is! Despite Risa's protests, Mom has set her up with Tony—a stockbroker. Much against Risa's better judgment, she meets Tony for a cocktail after work at a loud, smoky, downtown bar.

> TONY
> (Shouting over the din)
> Great place, hunghh?

> RISA
> What?

> TONY
> This is a great place!

> RISA
> There's something on my face?

Horrified, she puts her hands to her cheek.

> TONY
> (Leans close to her)
> I said—THIS IS A GREAT PLACE!

> RISA
> (Finally hears him)
> Oh. Yeah. Right.

TONY

The guys at the brokerage house go two places
when the market's up: here, or this happening
strip joint on lower Broadway.

RISA

Well I appreciate your not asking me to the
strip joint.

TONY

Yeah, well, some of the gals from work actually go there with us, if the market is up a
hundred or more.

RISA

That's—lovely.

TONY

So what did you say you do?

RISA
(Shouting back)
I'm a librarian.

TONY

Librarian? I didn't even know they still *had*
libraries.

RISA
(Under her breath)
What a surprise.

TONY

Hunghh?

RISA

I said it's a neat place to work.

TONY
(Scouting out other girls at the bar)
I bet. . . . Say, do you smoke cigars?

RISA
Me? You're joking, right?

TONY
Nahhh. Lots of girls do.

RISA
How—liberated—of them.

TONY
I'm going to get us a couple more beers. If I
got you a cigar, would you try one?

RISA
No thanks.

TONY
Oh. Well I'll get two anyway. We're going to
dinner at this really expensive steak house.
Maybe you'll want one there.

RISA
Look, Tony, can I ask you something?

TONY
Sure. Shoot!

RISA
Would you be terribly offended if I skipped
dinner and just said good night?

TONY
But you didn't even finish your beer?

> RISA
>
> I know. And I appreciate your going out with me. But I just think it's best we sort of call it quits now—while we're ahead.

> TONY
> (Amazed)
>
> Really?

> RISA
>
> Honest. I'm sure you're very nice and all, but I think I'll just go home—and read a good book. Do you mind terribly?

Tony's Take:

Believe it or not, even if he feels slighted at this particular moment, he's going to thank Risa in the morning for her honesty. You see, guys are a little slow on the uptake and don't always notice that a first date is turning into a real loser of a night. And besides, once they're on a date— even a bad one—they figure the worst they can do is try to have sex and call the evening a write-off. And that of course is the number one reason you see beers flying into guys' laps at singles bars.

BLIND DATE POINTER: If it is clear that this man you're with is an absolute zero, minimize your losses and walk out on the guy as soon as you can. Be polite, but be honest. Why leave any room for misinterpretation? It is a lose-lose situation for both of you.

Teaching An Old Dog New Tricks

The setup:

Crissy and Nick have been dating for about three months. They're getting along great and enjoying one another's company, but Crissy has one major complaint. It seems to her that every time they go out, they do the same thing. And Nick isn't exactly breaking any records for creativity. It's Friday night and they are on the phone deciding what to do.

> NICK
> (On Phone)

Hey, Crissy.

> CRISSY
> (On Phone)

Nick. Hey!

> NICK

Do we have a hot date tonight?

> CRISSY

I'm excited already. What are we up to?

> NICK

I was thinking maybe some beers after work with the guys, and then we could go over to Dirty Dora's?

> CRISSY
> (Less than enthusiastic)

Burritos? I was just thinking I could use a good bean load.

NICK
Great. Pick you up at seven?

CRISSY
Sure.

NICK
See you then!

CRISSY
(After a long pause)
Nick? Can I ask you something?

NICK
Of course. Fire away.

CRISSY
Could we maybe do something else tonight?

NICK
(Hurt)
Like what? You don't like my friends?

CRISSY
No, they're great guys. I love going out with
them. It's just, well, we always end up at
Dirty's with like twelve guys slamming pitch-
ers and eating 'til we can't move.

NICK
(Cheerfully)
I know. And great food, too!

CRISSY
I'll tell you what. Let's make a deal.

NICK
A deal?

CRISSY

Yes. I'd love to go out to Dirty's. We'll make it a big night. Invite everyone.

NICK

Sounds good.

CRISSY

But tomorrow night, you're mine!

NICK

Well that's appealing. Who brings the handcuffs?

CRISSY
(Petulantly)

I'm serious.

NICK

I'm sorry. So what are we doing tomorrow night?

CRISSY

I'm not going to tell you.

NICK

Well . . . what time? What should I wear?

CRISSY

Do you still own a suit?

NICK

Yes.

CRISSY

Remember how to tie a tie?

NICK
(Joking)
Not the opera. Please tell me you're not dragging me to an opera.

CRISSY
(Laughing)
I've just granted you your only wish. No opera. The rest of the night—you're mine!

Nick's Take:

This is a curveball he can live with. First of all, Crissy was gracious and delicate about expressing her need to occasionally have a night away from "the guys." Very important you try not to offend a man's buddies. Except for dogs, they're his best friends. Secondly, she offered a great alternative to the usual fare. She's taking charge. Guys love when you occasionally grab the reins. It takes the responsibility off of our shoulders and there is great potential for fun we haven't thought of before. Nice move, Crissy!

Check Please!

The setup:

Jason and Donna are casual acquaintances who met through work and are out on a first date. They started their evening with a cocktail at a nice bar and now they're finishing dinner. The waiter has just left them with the check.

JASON
So we hitchhiked all through Alberta for two
weeks until we met this Indian backcountry
guide who agreed to take us on a three-day
fishing trip—
(Picks up the check, examining it)
—but you know, it was already September and
they were starting to get snow in the mountains and I was sort of worried about the
weather—

DONNA
(Nabs the check)
Here. Let me.

JASON
No. Please. My treat. . . . Anyway, we set off
with this guide and wouldn't you know it, the
first night—

DONNA
No. I insist. Check's mine.

JASON
Please. No. I got it. . . . So the first night we
have a foot of snow. And I have nothing but
shorts and a summer sleeping bag—

DONNA
(Grabs the check)
I don't want you to buy me dinner!

JASON
(Grabs it back)
It's no problem!

DONNA

It *is* a problem. If you want to split it, that's
fine, but I don't let first dates buy me dinner!

JASON
(Totally off his story now)
You don't?

DONNA

No. Never!

JASON

Why not?

DONNA

That's none of your business.

JASON

Excuse me?

DONNA

I don't feel I owe you any explanation for why
I don't want men buying me meals.

JASON
You're dead right. Pardon me for living.

DONNA
(Calculating the tip on her pocket tip
calculator)
Now you were saying about the mountains or
snow or something?

JASON

Ahh, forget it.

DONNA
No. Really! I'm interested.

JASON

It was nothing. We had a blizzard, three of my friends and the Indian guide perished, and I lost four toes. . . . Maybe we should call it a night?

Jason's Take:

One: Never date a woman who carries one of those tip calculators. Two: Be wary of women who will break three of your fingers before they'll let you buy them dinner. That's straight from the guy-file! The days when a man "expected" something in return for picking up the tab are ancient history. We buy dinner because we enjoy the dating ritual—nothing more. We don't mind your offering to split the check or buy the next round. But starting an international crisis because a man wants to shell out fifty bucks is just not necessary, or fun.

FREE ADVICE: A man actually likes it when a woman takes him out. If you arrange the date and you want to pay for the evening, announce it! "Hey, Bill—I'm taking *you* out tonight. My treat!" That spares both parties any awkwardness, but still allows the man the chance to offer to buy a round—if you'll let him.

Dating Swine

The setup:

Stan and Judy are out on a first date. They were set up, so they don't really know a lot about each other. They've been to a so-so movie and Judy is not feeling much chemistry, but they'd already made dinner reservations so she's trying to give Stan a chance. Their dinner table is situated close to the bar, which happens to be heavily populated with singles. Stan seems to have his eye more on the bar than on Judy.

> JUDY
> . . . So we're just about to land when there's this big roar and a whooosh and everyone on the plane screams because we think we're about to crash. I mean I really thought it was all over. . . . Hello, Stan. Do you know someone at the bar?

He hasn't heard one word of Judy's story.

> STAN
> (Turns his attention back to her)
> Oh, no. Just looking. So did the plane crash?

> JUDY
> (With utter distaste)
> Yeah. It crashed. Everyone was killed except for me.

> STAN
> (Laughing)
> Ah ha ha. You're really funny. How's your salmon?

> JUDY
> Dry as toast. Truly awful.

> STAN
> (Not paying attention)
> Great. Did I tell you I used to date another stewardess?

> JUDY
> (Feigning interest)
No! Really? What airline?

> STAN
Don't remember. But she was some kind of fun, let me tell you.

> JUDY
I don't think I want to know.

> STAN
> (Actually apologizing)
I'm sorry. I didn't mean that all stewardesses are easy.

> JUDY
You're so charitable. And by the way, no one has called a "flight attendant" a stewardess in about twenty years.

> STAN
Oh c'mon. They don't mind when you call them that.

> JUDY
Maybe the "fun" ones don't.

The waiter comes over at that moment.

> WAITER
How's everything?

> JUDY
This fish should be in a museum. You can take it away. Just bring us the check.

> **STAN**
> The check? It's awfully nice of you to pick up
> dinner.

> **JUDY**
> (Can't believe him)
> The only thing I'm going to pick up is that
> plate of fries—and dump it on your head.
> Good night!

Stan's Take:

With any luck he'll get the subtle hint that Judy doesn't
like him. The fact is, not enough girls walk out on first
dates. That's how some guys turn into pigs. Maybe, if
Stan is not completely dense, Judy's storming out will
impart a valuable dating lesson—act like a buffoon and
you'll end up spending a lot of Saturday nights alone.

The Aspiring Chef

The setup:

Marc is preparing a fancy and somewhat challenging dinner for Meg at his apartment. They are drinking wine,
and conversation is tripping along at a brisk clip while
he serves the main course.

> **MARC**
> (Pot holders in hand)
> . . . So since my dad was in the foreign ser-
> vice, we lived in about nine different countries
> when I was growing up—and I guess that's
> where I got my love of food.

MEG

I think that is so neat. We traveled, too. The
Grand Canyon. Disney World. The Great
Lakes. That's where I got my love of—
McDonald's!

MARC
(Coming out of the kitchen with a
steaming casserole)
Well, I hope this holds a candle to a Big Mac.
Cassoulet. From scratch. Shall we?

He doles up two heaping bowls and arranges them on
the beautifully set table.
(Sets it down with a flourish)

MEG
(Raising her glass)
To the chef?

MARC
To you. For giving me an excuse to make a
nice dinner.

They clink glasses and Marc politely waits for Meg to
taste.

MEG
(Mouthful of hot food)
Hmmm . . . hmmmm. Hmmm?

MARC
How is it?

MEG
Ummmm? Hmmm. Ahhhh. Ohhhh—

MARC

What's wrong?

MEG

Uhhh, Marc?

MARC

Yes?

MEG

Did you use dried beans?

MARC

Of course.

MEG

Did you soak them?

MARC

Well, no. They were the quick boil type. . . .
Weren't they?

MEG

You try it.

MARC
(Samples the dish)

Arghhh.

MEG

I'm so sorry.

MARC
(Carefully removing a bean from his
jaw)

Rocks!

MEG
More like bullets I'd say.

MARC
(Crestfallen)
I am such a fool. These needed to soak over-
night. I've totally screwed it up—

MEG
Now stop that. Don't be silly.

MARC
I can't believe it. I am so embarrassed—

MEG
Marc—It's okay.

MARC
It is?

MEG
Well, no. The cassoulet tastes like buckshot
stew.

MARC
(Ruefully)
It's inedible, isn't it?

MEG
You could go rabbit hunting and use it for
ammo.

MARC
I'm really sorry.

MEG
I'm not. You tried and you blew it. I think
that's great.

MARC

You do?

MEG

Sure. We'll do it together next time.

MARC

But what about dinner now?

MEG

Well I *am* starving.

MARC

How about I take you out to a nice fancy restaurant. Anything you like!

MEG
(With a warm smile)
Is there a McDonald's around here?

Marc's Take:

How can you not love a woman like this? We invest so
much energy trying to woo you, impress you, and win
your respect, if not a little affection along the way. Marc
gave it his best shot with dinner, and totally messed it
up. Yet Meg found him charming, endearing, and good
company to boot. This is a terrific message to send a guy
who grabs your attention. It says you like him, you have
a sense of humor, and you can roll with the punches. And
that says to a guy, this is a woman for the long run!

Silence Can Be Golden

The setup:

Margaret and Justin are sitting at a play, between acts, on a first date. Margaret is regaling him with a story about her family. Justin sits dazed with a sort of glassy stare on his face, nodding occasionally to reassure Margaret he has not died during the intermission.

JUSTIN
So tell me again. Your half sister is a photographer in San Francisco and she lives with your real dad—

MARGARET
(Talking really fast)
No, my *real* dad died ten years ago. I just love Pete like my real dad. My real dad divorced my mom when I was a kid and then, well, he died a year later. So I never knew him. But my first stepdad always felt like my real dad—I mean, whatever you imagine a real dad might feel like. But I'm really closer to my mom anyway. So it's okay that my half sister gets more time with dad, because Mom and I get to take this trip to Florida together every year to visit my half brother from my mom's first marriage. And I'm really close to her! What about you?

JUSTIN
(Wipes his brow)
What about me?

MARGARET
Are you close to your family?

JUSTIN

Well, actually I am. We all like each other
pretty well. Last summer, as a matter of fact,
we took a family vacation at the shore—

MARGARET
(Interrupting)

Oh! That totally reminds me. Did I mention
my dad's—well *step*dad's—third wife is the
mother of one of the stars of *Baywatch*? I met
him once on a trip to L.A. Very cool guy. I
started watching *Baywatch* after that. You
know, that's not such a bad show. People
really rag on it, but if you ever watched it,
you'd see it has some pretty good messages.
Do you ever watch TV?

JUSTIN

I like sports.

MARGARET

I used to date a guy who never turned off
ESPN. He was, like, insane about hockey. He
said he loved to have sex during it. Only it
wasn't with me, which now that I think about
it—what a bastard! You think he was cheating
on me and I didn't even notice?

JUSTIN

Well I'm not Dr. Ruth or anything, but—

MARGARET

God guys can be such dogs. You know I once
brought a date home to my place and we had
a couple of beers with my roommate and I
went to the bathroom and when I came out he
was getting her work number to ask her out.

Which I guess doesn't say much about my
roommate either. Do you have a roommate?

JUSTIN
No. I live in a small studio over on—

MARGARET
(Totally cuts him off)
You are so lucky. The rent in the city is just a
killer. I'd love to have my own place. Of
course I'd need about twice the salary I get
now, which isn't likely considering my boss.
Who happens to hit on me every day. I don't
mean like sexual harassment or anything, but
he drops these comments—and it's like, you
know. That happened to one of my other step-
sisters. The one who works in sales. Boy, did
she ever get into a jam. Did I tell you about
Candy, my second stepdad's daughter from
his first marriage?

Justin's Take:

"No, and if you don't clam up for a second, I'm going to
walk out of this theater, leave a tape recorder, and call you
in the morning for the transcripts!" That's about where Justin is on this date about now. Why do women (and no
doubt men) sometimes run off at the mouth for unendurable
stretches? Because we're nervous. But that doesn't make it
fun, or right. Men love when women talk on dates. We
really do want to hear your tales. But occasionally come up
for air and see if your date is still there. If his eyes are
glazing over, it may be time to take a breather!

FREE ADVICE: Complex family tales, deep psychological
problems, and any story that ends with the words, "I

guess you had to be there," are bad news on first dates. Stick to job, sports, the weather, college, mutual friends, or recent travels. See where the yarns take you. No one— man or woman—enjoys being on one end of a windy monologue.

A Woman of Compassion

The setup:

Brad and Wendy have been dating for a few months, long enough that they can share in some of the decision- making process when it comes to where they go and what they do on dates. Brad has taken Wendy to a new, highly reviewed restaurant that has drawn a large and oh-so-chic crowd. After waiting about three days, they are finally seated.

> BRAD
> You don't still feel faint, do you?

> WENDY
> No, the peanuts at the bar helped.

> BRAD
> Good. I'm really sorry that took so long. I guess reservations don't mean much these days.

> WENDY
> Hey. At least we're here. You think we'll get a menu before the year 2000?

Several more minutes go by and finally a waiter shows up and disdainfully lays down two menus.

BRAD
(To the departing waiter)
Hey, hang on. We'd like to order a bottle of
wine—
(Brad quickly peruses the wine list)
—Jeez Louise. Ummmm—

WENDY
(Taking the lead)
How about two glasses of the house cabernet?

WAITER
(Exiting)
Of course.

BRAD
You didn't have to do that.

WENDY
Oh come on. Look at this list. You'd have to
take out a mortgage for the cheapest bottle.
Who needs that. Let's order.

They start to read the menu and grow awfully quiet.

BRAD
(Sort of sick at what he sees)
Order whatever you want.

WENDY
(Cheerfully)
Right. Hmmmm. Well, we can share an
appetizer.

BRAD
No. That's okay. Do you know what you're
going to have?

WENDY

Bread will be fine to start. Honest. If they ever bring any. . . . What are you going to have for dinner?

BRAD

Well, let's see. Ummm, the spaghetti à la buerre de poivre sounds good.

WENDY

Brad?

BRAD
(Getting in a bad mood)
What?

WENDY

Do you really want spaghetti with butter and pepper—for $23.95?

BRAD

Sure. It's exactly what I'm in the mood for. What are you having?

WENDY
(Leaning over)
Can I tell you what I want?

BRAD

Sure. Go ahead.

WENDY

I want to walk straight out of here, go to Tony's, get a pitcher and a large pie, then go back to your place and fool around! That's what I want.

BRAD
(Still sulking)
Oh, c'mon. I wanted to take you somewhere
special tonight. It's our three-month
anniversary.

WENDY
You're sweet. But do you really want to drop
150 bucks here?

BRAD
Actually—I'd like to drop the waiter from a
tall ladder!

WENDY
(Getting up)
Come on, big spender. We'll order the pie
with the works. I'll think you're Joe Cool. . . .

Brad's Take:

This is the kind of girl that makes dating a sheer joy. The
kind you fall in love with for absolutely no reason, and
every reason! It's hell being a guy and carrying the weight
of the dating load at the beginning of a relationship. When
a woman shifts gears to becoming a partner—not just a
dinner tab—it tells the guy that she likes being with him.
Doesn't want to see him spend foolishly. Doesn't want
him to feel like he has to impress her. This is the stuff of
a growing and serious romance.

Chapter 3
GETTING INVOLVED

The Monday Morning Call

The setup:

Ed and Julia went out on their first big weekend date Saturday night. We're talking date number three, but really it's date number one (since dates one and two were just a drink after work and a weekday lunch date). Saturday night featured dinner, then dancing 'til 2:00 A.M., but no serious fooling around. Now it's Monday morning and Julia is hanging out at her desk talking to a friend when the phone rings. Guess who?

                    ED
              (On phone)
        Hello. Julia?

                    JULIA
              (On phone)
        Yeah. Hi Ed.

(Whispers to her friend)
It's him. I'll talk to you later.
(Back to Ed)
How you doin'?

ED
Good. How about you?

JULIA
I'm great. Is your back feeling better?

ED
Yeah. I guess I got sort of excited on the dance
floor. Is your wrist okay?

JULIA
It's fine. I just wish I had caught you a little
better. That was scary the sound your head
made when it hit the floor. . . .

ED
Well at least neither of us ended up in the
hospital.

JULIA
I always call that a plus on a date.

They both laugh.

ED
That *was* a pretty nice date, wasn't it?

JULIA
Yeah. I had fun.

ED
Me too.

JULIA

So you got a busy week ahead?

ED

Nothing too heavy. How about you?

JULIA

I'm around.

ED

Hey, look. I know it's Monday morning and all and you probably haven't even had your coffee yet, but I was wondering—

JULIA

I'd love to.

ED

But I haven't even asked you yet?

JULIA

Well, go ahead.

ED

Uhhh, want to do something one night this week?

JULIA

Let me check my calendar. Okay.

ED

Should I take that as an enthusiastic yes?

JULIA

You had 'til noon before I bitched to my girl-friend or called you myself.

ED
Well, good thing I called when I did. How's
Wednesday night?

JULIA
Count me in. Seeya. . . .

Ed's Take:

Surprise, surprise—guys can be insecure, too. Here's what
we can glean from eavesdropping on this phone call. Fun
was had by both. Ed is a horrible dancer (as are 99.6
percent of all men.) And mercifully, Julia thought it was
cute. She was delighted to hear from him after their Saturday night together and made no bones about it. Score
her a ten for compassion (putting up with Ed's abysmal
footwork) and for showing just the right amount of enthusiasm to want to go out again.

BROWNIE POINTS: When Julia asked Ed if he had a
busy week ahead, she basically opened the door for him.
No woman asks a man a question like that unless she
wants in on that busy schedule. Great ploy to get a guy
to ask you out sooner, not later!

Give Him a Hand

The setup:

Dave and Sharon have been dating nearly a month, with
no "action" whatsoever. A couple of lunches, a few movies and dinners, all-in-all pleasant dates with nothing
more than a good-night kiss. It's Saturday night and once
again they are having a fine evening. A good movie fol-

lowed by a long, lingering dinner and now they've opted
to continue the date at a neighborhood pub. It's past midnight, the kind of date where a guy is either having a
great time or has something else on his mind.

                    DAVE
        (Brings back two pints of Watney's)
        This okay?

                    SHARON
        Absolutely. I love British beer. I lived in En-
        gland for a semester junior year.

                    DAVE
        No kidding.

                    SHARON
        Yeah. It was great. I was studying English lit
        at Cambridge.

                    DAVE
        Wow. Sounds serious.

                    SHARON
        Don't be fooled. Me and my best girlfriend
        traveled all over England, Scotland, and Wales
        for three months—and snuck a few classes in
        between.

                    DAVE
        Now that's the way to do junior year abroad.

                    SHARON
        I'll say. What about you? Did you go abroad
        during college?

DAVE

Depends. If you consider ski bumming around
Wyoming abroad—

SHARON

That sounds fun.

DAVE

It was. Way too much fun. But you know, I've
never even been to Europe.

SHARON

Get outta here. You're kidding?

DAVE

Nope. I'm completely déclassé. Uncouth. Totally unsophisticated.

SHARON

Give me a break!

DAVE

Okay. Just a little behind the eight ball when it
comes to travel.

SHARON

So where do you want to go first?

DAVE

Well, London sounds good. I've always
wanted to see France and Germany. Oh, and
Italy of course.

SHARON

Sounds like a plan to me. When are we going?

Dave very nonchalantly reaches down and *holds Sharon's
hand*.

> DAVE
> Well, let's see. We've got that weekend in
> Maine we talked about. And San Francisco is a
> must.

> SHARON
> (Playing along—and still holding his
> hand)
> Of course.

> DAVE
> You said you love Cape Cod.

> SHARON
> Any day, any time.

> DAVE
> Well, sounds like we're pretty busy through
> the summer. How about two weeks by train
> through Europe in the fall?

> SHARON
> (Squeezing Dave's hand)
> That sounds really nice.

They look into each other's eyes, the way people do when
something wonderful is about to happen. Their hands fold
and entwine, getting to know each other's "feel."

Dave's take:

He's falling, head over heels! Believe it or not, a guy gets
tingles down his spine, too, the first time he holds hands
with you. What's more, it is equally as scary to take your
hand as it is to, say, kiss you the first time. What if you
drop his hand like a cold fish? What if you pull back in
horror? What if you ask: "What the heck do you think

you're doing?'' (Yes, we've had that happen, too!) A nice hand-holding moment before any real intimacy is a great sign to a guy with serious intentions. It says you like him, and it gives him the right kind of signals that perhaps a little more fun might be in order soon.

Wedding "Date" Blues

The setup:

Kirk and Samantha have been dating quite a while, nearly a year. One of Samantha's best college buddies is getting married and Samantha is in the wedding party. However, for the third wedding in a row Kirk balks at going, and Samantha is starting to wonder why.

> KIRK
> I've never even met this person, Sam. Why do you want me to go the wedding of a person I've never even met?

> SAMANTHA
> Gambril and I were best friends junior year.

> KIRK
> That was six years ago.

> SAMANTHA
> You still go out with *your* college friends all the time.

> KIRK
> I still *talk* to my college friends all the time.

SAMANTHA
(Growing resentful)
I talk to Gambril a lot.

KIRK
Yes, I know. Ever since she asked you to be in
her wedding. The color of the dress, the color
of the shoes, the color of the handbag . . . the
bridal shower, the bachelorette party, the re-
hearsal dinner. Is this going to be, like, the so-
ciety wedding of the year or something?

SAMANTHA
No, lamebrain. It's just a regular old wedding.
You know, the kind where the bride wears a
white dress and all her friends walk down the
aisle in something peach—and the brides-
maids' boyfriends watch lovingly from the
pews and then race for a beer after the
ceremony?

KIRK
Well that sounds really fun. Except I've never
met the bride, and I've never met any of the
bride's friends. So I get stuck sitting next to
Aunt Gertie while you're yukking it up with
all your pals.

SAMANTHA
If you'd come to the other weddings I invited
you to, you'd know all of these people.

KIRK
I didn't think you wanted me at the other weddings, with your old college boyfriend there
and all.

SAMANTHA
(Changing her tune)
Kirk. Sweetheart? You know I wanted you
there. Are you jealous of my old college
boyfriend?

KIRK
(Grumpy)
Of course not! You want me to come to this
wedding?

SAMANTHA
More than anything.

KIRK
You're not going to leave me alone with Aunt
Gertie?

SAMANTHA
Are you kidding? You're going to look so
handsome in a tux I'm not going to let any
woman get near you. Especially crazy ol' Aunt
Gertie!

Kirk finally breaks down with a hint of a smile.

Kirk's Take:

Looks like he's going to a black-tie wedding. Begrudg-
ingly, but he's going. Weddings are one of those curiosi-
ties that really differentiate the sexes. Women seem to
take to the whole process, whereas men—especially
young ones—avoid it like the dentist. The way to get a
guy to a wedding is simple—promise him the world. Beer,
limousines, sex in the hot tub at the cheesy motel where
you and your college friends are all staying. Anything to
make the experience fun, and remind him—he's not re-

quired to ask you to marry him just because he's your wedding date!

Workingman Blues

The setup:

Cheryl and Todd have been going out for nine months. Todd is an overworked sixth-year associate at a law firm. Cheryl is a sales rep for a fancy line of clothing. While their relationship has been comfortable, it hasn't grown much in the past few months. And to complicate matters, Todd is working himself half to death, trying to make partner at his firm. It's Tuesday night—and it happens to be Cheryl's birthday.

>   TODD
>   (On Phone)
>   Cheryl?

>   CHERYL
>   (On Phone)
>   Hi, Todd. You almost done at work? I want to
>   go home and change before we go out.

>   TODD
>   Yeah. Right. Look, I've got some bad news.

>   CHERYL
>   What?

>   TODD
>   You're going to kill me.

CHERYL

You're blowing me off for my birthday.

TODD

I'm not "blowing you off." I made reservations and everything. I have a problem.

CHERYL
(Wearily)

And what is that?

TODD

You know that deal I'm working on with
those people in Florida? They just called and
they need it redrafted.

CHERYL

So?

TODD

So they need it tomorrow.

CHERYL

So you *are* blowing me off!

TODD

I just don't think we're going to be able to
make a nine o'clock dinner reservation.

CHERYL

Do you want to change it?

TODD

No. I think I'll be working until at least midnight. I was wondering if you want to go to
that all-night French café you like, instead, for
a late birthday supper.

CHERYL
No, Todd. I don't. I was really looking forward to dinner at Aja's.

TODD
So was I. But I can't very well tell the client to stuff it. This is my partner year, Cheryl.

CHERYL
This is my birthday, Todd.

TODD
(After a long pause)
Well, what do you want me to do?

CHERYL
(Long sigh)
I don't know. You're really going to work all night?

TODD
I don't have a choice. I'd really like to see you, even if it's for a late supper. It's up to you—

CHERYL
I don't know, Todd. I've got to think about it. Let me call you back. . . .

Todd's Take:

Cheryl's behavior is a bad harbinger for their relationship. You can call him a creep for working late on her birthday, but look at the situation. Is he supposed to lose his job or compromise his career ambitions because it's her birthday? Men know that plenty of women like guys who make the big bucks. It's a fact of life. But generally speaking, big bucks come with a price—lots of hours in the office. If you like dating a young man with a booming career, be prepared for the trade-off—quite a few nights keeping the sheets warm while he burns the midnight oil.

Recipe for Romance

The setup:

Reg shows up at Sandy's house to pick her up for a Saturday night date. He thinks he's taking her out to the movies and dinner, but she meets him at the door in jeans and a T-shirt—clearly not dressed for a night on the town. Apparently she has something else on her mind.

> REG
> Hey. Am I too early?

> SANDY
> Not at all. I just decided I wasn't in the mood for anything fancy tonight.

> REG
> That's cool. We can just grab a burger.

> SANDY
> I sort of had something else in mind. Would you mind doing something different?

> REG
> Sure. Why not? What's cooking?

> SANDY
> Well, that's sort of what I wanted to do.

REG

Hunhhh?

SANDY

Cook. You know, like cook dinner together.

REG

Really?

SANDY

Yeah. Would you mind?

REG

Well, I'm not the world's greatest chef. I make
a pretty good grilled cheese and bacon. . . .

SANDY

I think we can aim a little higher than that.
You like pasta, right?

REG

Of course.

SANDY

Maybe a chicken dish?

REG

Why not.

SANDY

A nice salad?

REG

Sounds great. You got all this stuff in your
fridge?

SANDY
(Jokingly)
No meathead! We have to go buy it!

REG
Wow, like at a store?

SANDY
Yes, Reg. Like at a store. Have you ever been to a grocery store?

REG
I used to like going when I was a kid.

SANDY
(Rolling her eyes)
Is this a horrible idea? Because if it is, we can go back to the burger and movie plan.

REG
(Smiling)
Sandy—I would love to make dinner with you. Honest!

Reg's Take:

Okay, Sandy caught him a bit off guard. But hey, this is a good thing. Men can stand a little confounding. Obviously, if a guy already cooks, he's going to consider your invite a suggestion for a more intimate evening—cramped little kitchens are great places to get to know one another. And if he doesn't cook very often, then this can be fun for both of you. It's not the menu that's key, but the fact that you've suggested the kind of date that leads down a new path— and new paths in a fresh relationship are a very good thing.

FREE ADVICE: The first time you cook dinner for a new

boyfriend, go easy on the epicurean difficulty scale. Two reasons. One, you don't want to spend three hours sweating over a French cookbook. And two, how many guys really appreciate a five-course French dinner? Better he be imagining you naked over pasta primavera, than putting out the fire you started when you tried to clarify butter!

Kissing Cousins

The setup:

Natalie and Sam have been great pals for several years. They hang out together all the time, set one another up on dates, and bemoan the miserable state of dating when both of their calendars are empty. On this particular Saturday night, they are sharing a pizza, just about ready to pop in *Sleepless in Seattle* for the fourth time in six months (*When Harry Met Sally* was out, as usual).

> SAM
> You know, I heard that there are people who actually "live" their lives, instead of watching it pathetically parodied in bad romantic comedies?

> NATALIE
> Do we actually know anyone who *has* a romantic life?

> SAM
> Bill and Katy are still an item.

> NATALIE
> That's true. Margie and Mike are engaged.

SAM
That was a good setup on your part. I never would have picked those two in a million years.

NATALIE
Yeah well, that's why they say men are blind.

SAM
Linda and Connor are still together.

NATALIE
Maybe, but I don't think they're long for this world. The only thing keeping them together is sex.

SAM
I once read that sex is supposed to be fun.

NATALIE
Especially when it's not by yourself.

SAM
Please don't talk dirty. I don't know if I can contain myself.

NATALIE
I'm not talking dirty. You know women don't masturb—

SAM
Don't say the "M" word. I'm dying here.

NATALIE
(Laughing at him)
You want to excuse yourself before the movie?

                              SAM
Nahhhh. I'll survive. I'm aiming for a new record.
Thirty-seven straight weekends without a date.

                            NATALIE
What am I? Chopped liver? Maybe I'll start
spending my Saturday nights with someone else.

                              SAM
Oh, come on, Nat. You've never even looked at
me cross-eyed. Not once since the day we met!

                            NATALIE
How do you know?

                              SAM
You think we'd be sitting here watching *Sleepless in Seattle*—again—if I didn't think you'd
burst into laughter if I tried to kiss you?

                            NATALIE
Well, you're probably right. Maybe if we
skipped the kissing part and just got into
bed—with very thick flannel pajamas on, of
course—we could wait and see what happens?

Sam's Take:

He is definitely considering that prospect at this very moment—and based on this conversation, probably not for the
first time. It's amazing how many "friends" get along better
than most of the couples they know, and the only thing
preventing them from being a couple themselves is intimacy.
If a man jokes enough about how you two should be "more
than friends," the odds are he means it. You might want to
at least consider him in a different light. You already like
him and trust him. Could dating him be any worse than all

those loser guys you've dumped in the past? (However, proceed with caution. The drawback of dating a friend is the risk of losing a friendship over a failed romance.)

INSIDE TIP: No matter how many times a male friend says he could never imagine kissing you, don't believe it. We are creatures of fantasy, and even our best girl "friends" fall into the category of potential lovers. You are usually no more than two beers and a moment's worth of courage away from being kissed by your best male friend!

Hold Your Horses Harry

The setup:

Adam and Cindy have been on four dates. Adam has been single for a while, but Cindy is just getting over a three-year romance. Adam is clearly into her. He's called after each date and asked her out again, sent flowers, and even managed to keep his libido more or less in check. They're standing at Cindy's doorstep after a nice evening, and Adam is attempting to kiss her rather passionately, obviously hoping for an invite into her apartment.

> CINDY
> (Resisting his smooches)
> Adam. Adam. Adam, please!

> ADAM
> Sorry. I was just, well. Whoops. Sorry.

> CINDY
> That's okay. It's just been a while since I've done this with someone new.

ADAM
(Jokingly)
And what better way to jump back into the
deep end—

He starts kissing her again. She gamely makes out for a
second and then pushes him away.

CINDY
I just can't do this.

ADAM
I think you're doing great.

CINDY
No, I mean I like you and all, but I'm just not
ready for this.

ADAM
Ready for what?

CINDY
I'm not sure. For getting involved.

ADAM
We don't have to get "involved" yet. We
could just make out and see what happens.

CINDY
I have a funny feeling what *you* want to happen and what *I* want to happen are two different things.

ADAM
(A little hurt)
But I thought we were having a good time?

CINDY

We were. I mean we are. And I like you, but this is just going too quickly.

ADAM

Kissing you good night is "too quickly"?

CINDY

No. I mean, yes. I mean, I don't know, Adam. I'm confused.

ADAM

About what? I really like you.

CINDY

I know. But maybe we should just chill out.

ADAM

What do you mean?

CINDY

I mean, like, not see each other—for a while.

ADAM

You mean like for a few days?

CINDY

No, I mean like this isn't such a good time for me right now. I told you I'm just getting over someone.

ADAM

You said that ended four months ago.

CINDY

Well it did, but I still . . . I mean . . . I don't know. Maybe I'm just not ready to get into a new relationship right now.

ADAM
So you don't even want to go out with me
anymore?

CINDY
(Sadly)
I don't know what I want!

Adam's Take:

Nuclear science is easier for men to understand than the
whims of women—especially women just getting over a
boyfriend. Adam probably knows he hasn't done anything wrong. An attempted good-night smooch is hardly
a cardinal sin on a fourth date. But what should he make
of Cindy's protests? There's no hard, fast rule for keeping
a guy at bay when you're getting over someone. But you
have to at least address the issue. Tell him you like him
(if you do), but you need time. You don't need to ditch
a potential romance, but you do have to throw him a
bone—even if it's explaining to him why you need to
chill. The guy who really likes you will hang around for
a very long time, as long as he knows he has a chance!

Wandering Eyes

The setup:

Monica and Fred are on a weekend date, enjoying a walk
in the crowded park on a Sunday afternoon in summer.
They've been dating a couple of months and they're just
starting to get to really know one another. One problem:
Fred is guilty of the occasional case of leering. Monica

tries to ignore this for as long as possible, but her patience finally runs thin.

> FRED
> I tried rollerblading once. It was a real horror show. I'm all thumbs. Even my feet.
> (Something catches his eye)
> Wow, look at them?

> MONICA
> Who?

> FRED
> That couple. They're good!

A young couple is doing all sorts of backward roller-blade dancing. He looks like a hippie artist in baggy shorts and a dirty T-shirt. She looks like a page from a dirty magazine, in cutoff shorts and the world's skimpiest bikini top.

> MONICA
> What am I looking at?

> FRED
> (Re: the skaters)
> They're a good pair.

> MONICA
> Are you talking about *them*, or her?

> FRED
> (No clue)
> Excuse me?

> MONICA
> (Fed up with him)
> How about if I just take off my T-shirt and

bra? Would you stare at *me* like you just escaped from prison?

FRED
(Totally confused)
Well, yes. No. I mean I think you have a really great body—

MONICA
Drop dead, Fred!

FRED
Wha—?

MONICA
Forget it!

FRED
What'd I'd say?

MONICA
It's not what you said. It's what you're doing!

FRED
What am I doing?

MONICA
Checking out every babe who walks by. What do you have, radar vision or something?

FRED
I'm not checking out babes. I like being with you.

MONICA
There! You did it again!

FRED
I did not! What do you want me to do, put on
horse blinders?

MONICA
You know, that's a really good idea!

Fred's Take:

Like all men, he's going to claim innocence on this charge.
That's because we think you don't notice. It's a well-
known fact that men love to stare at women. We are visu-
ally oriented. But we also know you hate when we do it!
So we have developed superhuman muscles in our eyes
for peripheral vision. If Monica likes Fred's company,
she's smart to cuff him early on. Hopefully, now that he's
been warned, he'll cut it out and pay strict attention to
her. (Or at least work harder at masking his roving eye!)

Relationship Overload

The setup:

Trevor has been dating Jill for about two months. They've
been to bed a couple of times and their relationship is
moving along at what any guy would consider a pretty
average clip. They go out for a casual bite on a Monday
night, and surprisingly, end up making love. This is the
first sleepover party they've had on a weeknight. After
sex, they are lying in bed watching Jay Leno.

TREVOR
(With a naked Jill in his arms, in the
glow of the TV)
Well that was a pleasant surprise.

JILL
Yeah. This is kind of fun playing grown-ups.

TREVOR
It does sort of reek of our parents, doesn't it.
The only thing that's changed is Johnny
Carson.

JILL
So you don't mind me staying over tonight?

TREVOR
Of course not. Why would I mind you spending the night?

JILL
Well, you know, some guys freak out if a girl
gets in their "space."

TREVOR
No big deal.

JILL
I'm really glad. You've got a really neat apartment. Maybe this weekend I'll bring some
stuff over.

TREVOR
Excuse me?

JILL
You know, underwear, a toothbrush, and that
kind of thing?

TREVOR
(Suddenly not so sure)
Hmmm. I guess that would be okay.

JILL
I haven't been in a relationship like this in so
long.

TREVOR
(Confused)
Like *what*?

JILL
Well, you know. Serious! Like we actually
have some kind of future. You know what I
mean?

TREVOR
(Alarm bells clanging)
Umm, Jill?

JILL
You know, you haven't even told me about
your parents. Are they nice? I mean I'm sure
they must be.

TREVOR
They're—fine. Say, Jill, ummm—

JILL
Are they young or old?

TREVOR
In their fifties.

JILL
I knew it. That's so cool. I really think I want

to have kids when I'm young. How about
you?

TREVOR
Yeah, I guess so.

JILL
(Getting all worked up)
So what would you name your first baby?
Would you rather have a girl or a boy?

TREVOR
Jill! We used a condom.

JILL
Not right this second, silly. I mean, someday.
You *do* want kids, don't you?

TREVOR
(Gets out of bed)
Will you excuse me. I'm going to see if there's
any beer left in the fridge. . . . Want one?

Trevor's Take:

If there isn't any beer left in the fridge, he'll probably go
out and buy some. And change his address while he's at
it! Jill's enthusiasm is mountains over the top for only the
third or fourth time sleeping together. Guys don't think
"kids and marriage" that quickly (except with the girls
who *won't* sleep with them). We are evolutionary in our
mating habits. We need to grow into the idea that all this
time spent together is leading somewhere.

FREE ADVICE: Do not mention the following subjects
after sex with a boyfriend of six months or less: engage-

ment rings, children, station wagons, 401Ks, mortgages, fine china, wedding dresses.

Crossing Scary Bridges

The setup:

Thursday night. Sally and Walt are just wrapping up a dinner date and getting ready to call it a night. They've only been dating about a month so very little is etched in stone. Walt leans forward on his elbows, ready to pose the all-important question.

> WALT
>
> Say, Sally?

> SALLY
>
> Yeah?

> WALT
>
> I was wondering . . . ummm, how would you feel about spending the day Saturday?

> SALLY
>
> Spending the day?

> WALT
>
> Yeah. You know, like not doing anything. I mean, a bike ride or a picnic or a walk or a movie or I don't know what. Let's just get together and not make plans yet?

> SALLY
> (Hesitantly)
> Ummm, that sounds nice—

                    WALT
Great. How about if I meet you around ten
and we'll hoof it from there.

                    SALLY
                (Interrupting)
Uhh, Walt—

                    WALT
Wait for me for breakfast. We can at least plan
that much! And then the rest of the day we'll
do whatever you feel like—

                    SALLY
Wait a sec. Walt—

                    WALT
You want to go bowling, we'll go bowling.
Make a lasagna. We'll make a lasagna. Wind-
surfing? Antiquing? Renaissance Fair? You
name it!

                    SALLY
Walt! Hold the phone. I'd love to spend the
day with you. I really mean it.

                    WALT
But?

                    SALLY
But—there's a little problem.

                    WALT
                (Immediately hangdog)
Oh.

                    SALLY
How do I say this?

WALT
Just tell me. I'm tough.
(Jokes)
I'm a man.

SALLY
I've already got a date.

Dead silence. That went over really well!

WALT
(Suddenly embarrassed)
Okay. No problem. Sorry I asked.

SALLY
No. Wait. Walt? It's no big deal. Just some
guy who's been asking me out for months. I
finally said yes to him a few weeks ago. You
and I had only been out once then.

WALT
So you really hate him?

SALLY
I don't even know him.

WALT
But he's really ugly. And stupid? A real
knuckle-dragger?

SALLY
Do you think I would go out with someone
like that—
(Realizes she's being teased)
You're kidding, right?

> WALT
> (Sympathetic)
> You go on your date. I'll just do something else.

> SALLY
> You're not hurt?

> WALT
> No. Of course not. I'll just call my friend Cindy. I think you know her?

> SALLY
> I do?

> WALT
> Cindy Crawford!

They look at each other and smile.

Walt's Take:

Sally handled this potentially damaging situation beautifully. Three cheers for honesty. You should never lie to a man you may like. It can be very embarrassing if you run into him at the movies with your other date. What's more, by being straightforward about your plans, you've actually let on that you care for him. Why else would you be honest, unless you thought the other date was harmless. That's reassuring to us. It says you're a straight shooter and it says we're definitely in the running for your affections. This will surely inspire a call early Sunday morning, when we pray you'll be waking up alone and thinking deeply sexual thoughts about US!

Chapter 4
NOT JUST FOOLING AROUND

How to Send a Man Home

The setup:

Linda and Rick are making out in front of her apartment like there's no tomorrow. Lord knows what they did on their date earlier in the evening, but at this particular moment one gets the feeling that this is a tinderbox waiting to ignite. Hands are exploring various places and Rick suggests they move the activity inside. Linda undoes a couple of buttons on Rick's shirt, starts playing with his chest, then slowly buttons his shirt back up.

> RICK
> So should we go in for a nightcap—or something?

> LINDA
> What "or something" did you have in mind?

RICK
Well, it's your place, so I thought you might
have a few ideas.

LINDA
I do! Quite a few. Except for one little
problem—

RICK
(Groaning)
Your roommate's home.

LINDA
No. Actually she's in Atlanta for the weekend.

RICK
Ohhhh, there is a God.

LINDA
(Kisses him once more)
The problem is, this is only our third date.

RICK
(Responding to her kisses)
I know. Can you imagine our fourth?

LINDA
I am. And that's why I have to say good night
for now.

RICK
Good night?

LINDA
That's right. Good night.

RICK
You mean like "good night, just go home and

fill my bath with ice and jump into it because
I'm dying here?"

LINDA
If that's what turns you on. I personally plan on
taking a *warm* bath. You know, the kind where
you pour a glass of wine and slip out of your
clothes and think about how hot your body feels
while you slide naked into the water—

RICK
Arghhh! Stop. Don't use that word—

LINDA
What word?

RICK
Naked! I can't bear it.

LINDA
(Kissing him)
Are you wondering what I look like nak—

RICK
Don't say it.

LINDA
(Unlocking her door)
But you *will* be wondering?

RICK
You don't want to know what I'll be doing.

LINDA
Maybe I do.

With an evil wink she kisses him on the cheek and closes
the door.

Rick's Take:

He's going to go home and he's going to do something unspeakable. And he'll definitely call Linda again very soon. Why? Because she's sent him packing with more than just a raging physiological reaction—she's activated his brain! Suppose she did invite him in? They would have one of those nights guys dream about, and then the suspense would be gone. Instead, she gave him a farewell to remember, a tantalizing memory to carry around, and a promise she'll see him again. This is a win-win for everyone. They can cool their jets for a night, go out again, and when the moment is right, cut loose. Sending a guy home is not a crime when you do it right. It is an incredible enticement, and it can only build the romantic level to new heights.

How NOT to Send a Man Home (if you like him)

The setup:

Matt and Wanda are on a fourth date, and there seems to be a mutual attraction. Wanda invites him up to her apartment for a nightcap. She puts on some James Taylor, offers up a couple of beers, and joins Matt on the couch. The roommate is nowhere to be seen, the lights are low, and Wanda's acting pretty interested. Matt moves in for the kiss. She responds. Slightly. Matt turns up the heat. She responds. Slightly. Matt puts a hand somewhere it doesn't belong. Wanda shoves him away like he just tried acupuncture on her.

WANDA
(Indignant)
What do you think you're doing?

MATT
Uhhh, I was kissing you?

WANDA
No you weren't. I know exactly what you
were doing.

MATT
You do? What was I doing?

WANDA
Oh give me a break. Just because I invited you
in doesn't give you carte blanche to jump my
bones.

MATT
Jump your bones?

WANDA
Come on. Do I look like I was born yesterday?
I think you should go.

MATT
(Totally surprised)
Wanda! I thought we were having a good
time.

WANDA
Yeah. Me too. Just shows you how you can
misjudge someone.

MATT
I just kissed you!

WANDA
Oh stop it. You had your hands all over me.

MATT
I touched your back.

WANDA
You tried to unsnap my bra.

MATT
Through your shirt?

WANDA
Look, let's forget about it. I'm just tired of *every* guy expecting sex on a first date.

MATT
It's our fourth date.

WANDA
You know what I mean. Now really, please. Can we just say good night. No hard feelings?

Matt's Take:

No hard feelings? You can bet Matt's going home with hard feelings. Not because he had any sort of expectations, but because Wanda ambushed him with the frustration of her past dating experiences and gave him hell for it. How about a gentle "cut it out," or "please don't do that." Every woman has the right to stake out her space and make herself clear. And if the guy doesn't get the message, boot him out and burn his phone number. But don't blame every single guy for his predecessor's bad behavior. How can we possibly know what went on during your last dozen dates?

TRUE CONFESSION: Guys have feelings, too. The "nice guy" you've been waiting for is just as capable of getting hurt by rejection as you are. If he misreads your signals, or you're just not in the mood—tonight—let him know *gently.* The "nice guy" will respond in kind and come knocking again when the time is right!

Summer Nights on Front Porches

The setup:

Andrew and Leigh have been dating for about two months and the romantic attraction is strong, yet they have not so much as made out. Andrew has been respectful and kind almost to a fault, and Leigh is starting to wonder if anything is ever going to happen. They're just ending a date, and Leigh is about to go inside.

> LEIGH
> I had a really great night.

> ANDREW
> I did, too. I really enjoy the time we spend together.

> LEIGH
> Me too, Andrew.

They stand quietly in awkward silence. Something is supposed to happen here. Only it isn't.

> ANDREW
> Well, I guess I should be going.

> LEIGH
> Do you want to come in or something?

ANDREW
Well, it's kind of late. And I don't want to
wake your folks.

LEIGH
We could hang out on the porch swing for a
while. They'd never hear us. Their bedroom is
on the back of the house.

ANDREW
Well, you're probably tired.

LEIGH
Andrew?

ANDREW
Yeah?

LEIGH
You like me and all, don't you?

ANDREW
Are you kidding? I'm wild about you—I
mean, sure I like you Leigh.

LEIGH
Because I've really enjoyed our time together.

ANDREW
Me too.

LEIGH
So, ummm, can we get together again soon?

ANDREW
I'd like that. Maybe a picnic tomorrow?

LEIGH
That would be nice.

ANDREW
Okay.

LEIGH
Andrew?

ANDREW
(puzzled)
Yeah? Are you okay?

LEIGH
I'm fine. It's just . . . well . . . Andrew—

She impulsively takes him by the back of the head and plants a kiss on him that could weld nails. He responds. They kiss some more. . . .

LEIGH
(Coming up for air)
Ahhh. That's better. You can go now.

ANDREW
Hunghh?

LEIGH
Thanks for a great night.

ANDREW
(Totally confused now)
So do you still want to picnic tomorrow?

LEIGH
(Brightly)
Pick me up at noon sharp. Okay?

ANDREW
Uhh, yeah. Okay. Good night?

LEIGH
(Letting herself in)
Good night Andrew. Good night. . . .

Andrew's Take:

Wow! To have a girl take the lead and kiss you good night on her front porch—that's one great way to end a date. Why did it take Andrew so long that *Leigh* finally had to make the first move? Maybe he liked her so much he didn't want to blow it by rushing things. Maybe he's shy. Maybe he's the kind of guy who needs a really strong signal before he takes that first step. Giving a man an unexpected good-night kiss is one of the most exciting things a woman can do. It definitely sends him home smiling from ear to ear, counting the hours until he can see her again.

FREE ADVICE: When it comes to intimacy—any kind of intimacy—feel free to surprise him. Whether it's a stealth kiss or a squeezed hand or an unplanned attack in the front seat of his car, you just can't go wrong here. If he isn't feeling the attraction you are, he'll slow you down. And if he is, but he's been slow to act, then you're on your way to wherever the next step leads.

Creative Uses for a Bed 101

The setup:

On their fifth date, Fran, a reasonably cautious type, has somehow found herself in Nathan's bed, sort of fully, partially, kind of dressed. Nathan is in a similar state of being not exactly in bed, not exactly out. So here they are: both half-dressed and unsure where to go.

> FRAN
> I should probably be going.

> NATHAN
>
> Going where?

> FRAN
> (Putting her bra back on)
>
> Home?

> NATHAN
> (Slipping it off again)
>
> You can always make yourself right at home, here!

> FRAN
> Well, I gotta give you credit. You sure know how to make a girl feel at home, but I'm really not sure this is such a good idea.

> NATHAN
> Oh, I think it's working out quite nicely.

They start to go at it again. Fran is really in a quandary, not necessarily wanting to resist Nathan's advances, but not wanting to go a lot further along in the game.

> FRAN
> Nathan! What are you doing?

> NATHAN
> (Nuzzling her seductively)
> I believe I'm trying to drive you wild, so the

part of your brain saying "run" will lose out
to the part shouting "YES!"

                    FRAN
Is *that* it?

                    NATHAN
Yep. How am I doing?

                    FRAN
Too good. Maybe we should go back to the living room and watch TV or something.

Nathan halts in his seduction attempts, covers Fran's half-
naked body with her blouse, and leans back on his
elbows.

                    NATHAN
Okay. I've got a proposition.

                    FRAN
            (Smiles knowingly)
I can imagine.

                    NATHAN
No. That's not it. Will you listen if I make a
suggestion?

                    FRAN
I'll listen, but no promises.

                    NATHAN
Fair enough. Here's my offer. We get naked.
We get under the covers. You spend the night.
And I behave myself.

FRAN
(Laughing)
Behave yourself? Naked? You're kidding,
right?

NATHAN
I'm serious!

FRAN
We spend the night together. In your bed.
Naked. And you behave yourself?

NATHAN
That's right.

FRAN
Why do I have trouble believing this offer?

NATHAN
Because no guy has ever said that to you
before?

FRAN
Well that's true!

NATHAN
So waddaya say? Deal?

FRAN
(Her eyes light up)
Counteroffer. . . . We get under the covers. We
pick up where we left off. But you keep your
shorts on and I get your big ol' oxford shirt to
sleep in.

NATHAN
Underwear?

                      FRAN
        Depends.

                      NATHAN
        On what?

                      FRAN
                (Kissing him deeply)
        On whether I decide I can trust you . . .

Nathan's Take:

He's going to spend the night with Fran under the covers, in his shorts—or a ski parka if that's what it takes to keep her around! And he's going to do whatever she wants him to do, whenever she wants him to, for as long as she wants him to. That's because Fran turns him on, he likes her, and she boldly laid out her own ground rules for foreplay, without leading him on. Men are not solely climax-driven. We are very fond of all the steps leading to lovemaking and very patient about "going all the way." Nathan will be utterly, blissfully content holding her somewhat/maybe/partially clothed body all night. That's turn-on enough, until Fran decides it is time for more.

Crossing Signals

The setup:

Tana has invited Bob back to her apartment and they are fooling around big-time! The clothes are long scattered and they have explored most of the major positions without actually engaging in any indecent (or decent as the case may be) acts. Tana is positioned to perform oral sex, but Bob gently stops her.

> BOB
> No. Don't.

> TANA
> Hunghhh?

> BOB
> Hello. Come back here. Kiss me.

Tana happily obliges, then goes back to the previous task. Bob stops her again.

> TANA
> What's wrong?

> BOB
> Nothing. Absolutely nothing. This is—*you* are fantastic!

> TANA
> You're not half-bad yourself.

> BOB
> (Sits up in bed)
> Tana—

> TANA
> Yeah?

> BOB
> I'd really like to make love to you.

> TANA
> I'd like to make love to you, too.

She heads south again, but Bob stops her.

> TANA
> (Frustrated)
> What's wrong?

> BOB
> Nothing. I just don't want—*that*—right now.
> I'd really like to make love to you.

> TANA
> You mean, like, "make love"?

> BOB
> Yeah. That kind. Do you have any condoms
> here?

> TANA
> Of course. But I'm not going to do *that*.

> BOB
> Do what?

> TANA
> Make love!

Now Bob is a little confused.

> BOB
> I thought that's what we're doing?

> TANA
> I was going to give you a—

> BOB
> I know. And I'm not complaining. But I
> thought you wanted to—you know?

TANA

Bob. I hardly know you. We've only been dating like a month.

BOB

Well, yeah. But aren't we getting along here? I
thought we really liked each other.

TANA

We do. And I'd love to finish what I was
about to start . . . but I don't just make love to
anybody. That's really personal.
          (LONG PAUSE)
Hello, Bob? Anybody home? What's wrong?

Bob sits back in bed, the fire out. Tana looks absolutely
perplexed.

Bob's Take:

Don't fall off your chairs now, but Bob wasn't looking for
the quick fix of oral sex. Men don't always understand
how a woman can perform oral sex on a date, but not
engage in sexual intercourse. Of course if the guy is just
looking for gratification, he's not going to stop a woman.
But the man who really likes you—e.g., Bob—can actually
get his feelings hurt if a woman will perform oral sex,
but draw a big red line at making love. Some guys consider both acts deeply personal and intimate, and might
come away very confused if you'll happily do one while
firmly rejecting the other.

The Drill Sergeant

The setup:

Lesley and Duncan have been lovers for about a month, and while their lovemaking sessions have been athletic and satisfying, Lesley seems to be more the insatiable one. Still, Duncan is always willing to give it his best shot. On this particular Saturday night, they are in the middle of some heated foreplay.

> LESLEY
> Slow down, Duncan.

> DUNCAN
> I'm trying. There. How's that?

> LESLEY
> Just move your head a little.

> DUNCAN
> There?

> LESLEY
> Yes. No. Faster.

> DUNCAN
> You just told me to slow down.

> LESLEY
> No, that's good. That's really good.
> Long silence. Are things going well?

> LESLEY
> Why did you stop?

DUNCAN

Stop what?

LESLEY

What you were doing.

DUNCAN
(Sitting up)
I didn't stop anything!

LESLEY

Yes, you did!

DUNCAN
(Going back to work)
You're driving me crazy.

LESLEY

Me too, honey. There. That's great. No, not
like that. Like that!

DUNCAN
(Coming up for air)
Let's make love.

LESLEY
(All breathy)
Yes dear. In a second. Keep going. Wait. No.
There. Yes. Yes. No. Duncan. What are you
doing? Keep going. Don't stop. Come on. Yes.
No. No. Ohh, Duncan. You had it. Why did
you—ohh. Darnit! There. Yes. No. Wait. No.
Oh no. No. No . . . no. Forget it. . . .

DUNCAN
(Sitting up again)
What's wrong?

LESLEY
(Disappointed)
Nothing. Don't worry about it.

DUNCAN
Worry about what?

LESLEY
(Clearly unsatisfied)
Nothing. I'll survive. Why don't we just make
love and get it over with. . . .

Duncan's Take:

About right now he'd probably rather take a cold shower. It's
wonderful that Lesley is confident enough to express her very
intimate and specific desires. We applaud women for that and
are glad for the coaching. But when you turn a fun challenge
into a life-or-death task, sometimes the joy can go right out
the window. If you're interested in turning a novice boyfriend into a longtime lover, don't berate him to the point
of humiliation. He's not likely to come back and try again.

FREE ADVICE: When coaching a man to drive you to new
limits, try a positive approach. Make it sexy, talk dirty, steer
him in the right direction, coax him with your favorite explicit
sounds of joy. Just don't make it feel like the football coach
running a drill. Somehow the fun vanishes when a woman
makes her orgasm feel like a personal vendetta against the
male race.

A Hands-On Experience

The setup:

Jeff has been dating Liz for several months and the attraction is huge—and mutual. Only problem is that while Jeff has been aggressively pursuing a higher level of sexual activity, Liz has been cutting him off at the pass—usually after a hot and heavy necking session. Once again, Jeff finds himself parked on Liz's couch with his engines running and the car stuck in idle. Their clothes are in various states of unbutton, but still mostly on.

> JEFF
> (Hands all over Liz)
> Why don't we go to your room?

> LIZ
> I don't think that's such a good idea.

> JEFF
> I bet I can make it a great idea!

> LIZ
> I have no doubt you can. I'm just not ready to open that door yet. The bedroom door that is.

> JEFF
> (Resigned, sighing)
> If you say so. Can I use your bathroom for a second then?

> LIZ
> (Looking at him oddly)
> You're not going to do something disgusting in there, are you?

> JEFF
> Nope. Just a quick icy shower.

> LIZ
> (Kissing him)
> Hold off on the cold shower. Maybe I can do something to relieve your pain.

JEFF
(Joking)
Yes. Feel my pain. . . .

They fool around real hot and heavy for another moment and then Liz gets up abruptly. She runs out of the room and comes back a second later with a jar of cold cream.

LIZ
I'm back.

JEFF
What's that?

LIZ
Cold cream.

JEFF
Might I ask what for?

LIZ
You might not! Why don't you just cool your horses for a second and let me take charge here.

JEFF
What are you doing?

LIZ
(Smiling and fiddling with the button on his jeans)
A little something I'm sure you're very proficient at doing yourself.

JEFF
Well, isn't this exciting?

LIZ

I certainly hope so, or you don't have to come knocking at my door anymore.

JEFF

And to what do I owe this pleasure?

LIZ

Because I like you. And I want to be with you. And I can't bear to see you suffer anymore.

JEFF
(Sucking a deep breath)
I'm a very lucky guy.

LIZ
(Rubbing cream on her hands)
You don't even know the half of it. Just stick around. . . .

Jeff's Take:

Like he could even move off the couch at this exact moment? Liz has come up with the perfect (and oft-forgotten) solution to "overeager man meets let's-take-our-time woman." There are two ways to manually relieve a man in heat. One is to simply "give him a hand." The other is to turn the experience into an exciting one for both of you—making it more a part of foreplay than just a rushed ending to a long night. Men will love you for the special attention to their favorite solo act, and it keeps you high on the desire meter—until the time comes when we're both ready to go further into the mix.

Chapter 5
THE BIG STEP

How Did That Bra Get on My Lampshade?

The setup:

Stu and Mindy have not been dating very long. Maybe a few weeks, a handful of dates at most. On this particular Friday night one thing leads to another and next thing you know, Stu and Mindy are collapsed in a naked heap on Stu's couch at two in the morning, catching their breath. This turn of events was mutual and more than a little fun, but from Mindy's standpoint, definitely somewhat of a surprise.

> MINDY
> (Pulling a couch pillow over herself)
> Do you have a shirt or something I could put on?

> STU
> Umm, how about this?

He hands her his oxford shirt, which he picks up from the coffee table where it had recently been tossed.

                    MINDY
             (Covering herself)
So, uhhh, wow. You have a nice apartment.

                     STU
Thanks.
          (He pops on ESPN with the remote)
You been following the Cubs?

                    MINDY
Not really. I'm not too much of a sports fan.

                     STU
Oh.
          (Long awkward pause)
Say you wanna beer or something?

                    MINDY
Nahhh. Maybe I should be going.

                     STU
No-o-o. Gosh, you don't have to leave. Here. I
can turn off the game.

He pops off the TV, but Mindy is already getting dressed.

                    MINDY
I think I've had enough beers for one night.

                     STU
Is something wrong?

                    MINDY
No. Not really.

> STU
> C'mon. Something's bothering you.

> MINDY
> Well. You see, I don't usually do this—I mean not so soon at least.

> STU
> But you were great! Really great!

> MINDY
> Thanks. You were nice, too, Stu. But I don't even know you. And I think I should just be going.

She quickly finishes pulling herself together. Stu obliges by slipping on his boxer shorts at least.

> STU
> Can I walk you out?

> MINDY
> (In a pretty big hurry)
> Nahh, that's okay. Thanks for dinner, and the evening and all.

> STU
> Hey, Mindy?

> MINDY
> Yeah?

> STU
> I really do like you. I don't usually do this either.

> MINDY
> I'm sure.

STU

Can we go out tomorrow? Maybe brunch or something?

MINDY

I don't know. Maybe that's not such a good idea.

STU

Well can I call you?

MINDY

I guess so. Whatever. I really gotta go. G'night. . . .

Stu's Take:

He's genuinely sorry to see Mindy leave. Contrary to popular belief, men do not just want to get laid. They *are* capable of relationships that last fifteen minutes beyond orgasm. Mindy's behavior suggests she was very *un*comfortable with the fact that she did what she did. And this can make a guy feel like he's done something wrong, even if he didn't. Don't spend the night at his place if you aren't ready for that. But try not to race out the door and make the guy feel like he's committed a crime. You might accidentally send the wrong signal and jeopardize a potentially good romance before it's even had a chance to percolate.

Coitus Terrify-us

The setup:

Barbara and Chuck, who have been dating for about a

month have just made love for the first time. The sex was nice, all parties seemed reasonably satisfied, and it is clear that they are actually going to spend the night (as opposed to the midnight dash back to separate corners!). Chuck is settling in for a good, postorgasmic coma when Barbara leans up on her elbows with a determined look on her face.

> BARBARA
> You'll like my sister.

> CHUCK
> (Half awake)
> Excuse me?

> BARBARA
> My sister, Leah. She's, like, my best friend in the world.

> CHUCK
> Yeah. That's right. You did tell me about her. She sounds nice.

> BARBARA
> Maybe we can pop by her place tomorrow?

> CHUCK
> Hunghhh?

> BARBARA
> That is unless you want to meet her Sunday at dinner.

Now Chuck sits up in bed.

> CHUCK
> Sunday dinner?

BARBARA

At my parents' place. We always have family dinner at my parents' place on Sundays.

CHUCK
(Less than enthusiastic)
That sounds . . . nice.

BARBARA

So do you want to see a movie or something, before. I heard that new Stallone thriller is pretty good. Though to be honest, I prefer romantic comedies—

CHUCK

Before what?

BARBARA

Hunghh?

CHUCK

See a movie before what?

BARBARA

Dinner at my family's.

CHUCK

I'm sorry. Did we make a date for Sunday?

BARBARA

Well no, but—

She looks around, like, "duhhh, we *are* in bed!"

CHUCK

Ummm, Barbara, I'm sure your family is terrific and all, but I sort of have plans already.

BARBARA
Oh. Well that's okay. We can do it next
Sunday. . . .

Chuck's Take:

Help! Did Chuck just have sex on a fourth date or sign a
prenuptial agreement? This may sound cold, but the fact
is, just because a man has sex with you it does not mean
you are necessarily in a relationship. It might mean you
are on your *way* to a relationship, but guys move much
more slowly in this department. A surefire way to freak
a guy out is to make bold assumptions after the first time
you make love.

FREE ADVICE: The first time you sleep with a man you're
dating, admit exactly *half* of whatever you're thinking. If
it was the best sex you've ever had, tell him it was nice.
If being in his arms makes you feel like you want to spend
the rest of your life in that very spot, get up and go to
the bathroom. If he's so wonderful you feel the need to
make love four more times that evening, do it only twice.
Don't give away the farm on the first night in bed. There's
plenty more time to cultivate all the good things you
want—if and when it's right!

Hate to Eat and Run, But . . .

The setup:

Connie has just made love to Pete (and vice versa) for the
first time. Not surprisingly, Pete has fallen sound asleep
eighteen seconds after orgasm (male reflex). They are at
her apartment. Connie rather adoringly strokes his slightly

bearded face, and he wakes up suddenly, completely disoriented.

                    PETE
            (Sits up abruptly in bed)
Where am I?

                    CONNIE
Hey-y-y. Take it easy. It's me. Connie.

                    PETE
            (Getting his bearings)
Right. Connie! Hi.

                    CONNIE
Hi, Pete. That was really great.

                    PETE
Yeah. It was, wasn't it?

                    CONNIE
It sure was. I haven't done that in a long time.

                    PETE
            (Uncertainly)
Umm, yeah, me neither.

                    CONNIE
Hey, can I get you a beer or something?

                    PETE
That's okay.

                    CONNIE
            (Fumbling for her remote control)
You wanna watch *Saturday Night Live*?

> PETE
Umm, nahhh. You know—

> CONNIE
Me neither.
>   (Curls up tight with him)
I just like being with you.

> PETE
Yeah.

Clearly this date is not rocking.

> CONNIE
>   (Yawning)
Say, I'm going to brush my teeth. You don't
mind sharing toothbrushes, do you?

> PETE
Well actually—

> CONNIE
>   (Hopping out of bed)
Let me just pee first.

> PETE
>   (Also gets out of bed)
Uhhhh, Connie? I think I'm, uhhh, going to
head out.

> CONNIE
Head out?

> PETE
I mean, head home.

                    CONNIE
You don't have to go. My roommate is away
for the weekend. I told you that.

                    PETE
I know. But, ummm, I really should be going.

                    CONNIE
Why?

                    PETE
Because, uhhh, because—Well, I just sleep better in my own bed.

                    CONNIE
                (Seductively)
Well, we don't have to go to sleep yet.

                    PETE
I know. But honest, I think I better be going.

                    CONNIE
I don't get it. How come?

Pete's Take:

"Because I'm not ready for this kind of postcoital intimacy. At least not yet . . ." There. A male truth out in
the open. When a guy starts hoofing excuses to get out
of your apartment after you've made love the first time—
be warned. Either he has another girlfriend, or he may
not be very interested in a lasting relationship. We have
not yet learned the right way to excuse ourselves from
your boudoir, *after* making love. So the guy who wants
to leave will find an excuse, any excuse ("Haven't fed
my tarantula today!") to hit the road. While this may be
inherently insulting, it may also be the quick and easy

"out" for you, too. If he is that eager to leave, do you really want to invest in a future with this guy?

Once Might Have to Be Enough

The Setup:

Ray has been courting and attempting to seduce Randi for almost six months, and she's just made love to him for the first time. If anyone were keeping score, Ray would have given Randi a 10+, but as it turns out, Randi probably would have given Ray a 6 (and maybe a few bonus points for trying hard!) Now Ray is lovingly stroking Randi's long, pretty hair. She is actually starting to stroke something else.

> RAY
> You were really fantastic.

> RANDI
> (Jokingly modest)
> Thanks. 'Tweren't nuthin!

> RAY
> It was the most fun I've had in about four hundred dates. How about you?

> RANDI
> It was, uhhh, really nice.

She starts to administer some fairly serious attention to stoking Ray's fires again.

> RAY
> Ooh. Ahh. Careful.

RANDI
Whoops. Sorry. Am I hurting you?

RAY
Just a little sensitive still.

RANDI
Ahhhh. I'll be gentle. How's this?

She tries a new and seductive tack.

RAY
(Pushing her away)
Can we just—take it easy for a little bit?
Maybe rest a while?

RANDI
I'm not tired.

RAY
I can see that. But I need a little breather here.

RANDI
(Crawls down on him)
Maybe this will put some wind in your sails—

RAY
Randi! Please.

RANDI
What?

RAY
Can we just—lie here for a while?

RANDI
Is that what you brought me over for?

                         RAY
        Hunghhh?

                         RANDI
        Just to lie here?

                         RAY
        Well, no. Obviously—

                         RANDI
        So c'mon. The night's young.

                         RAY
        Are we rushing somewhere?

                         RANDI
        Apparently you were—a couple of minutes
        ago!

Ray's Take:

Game. Set. Match! If Randi had any intentions of courting
a lasting romance with Ray, her one little jab just nixed
that idea for the next ten trysts. If there is anything in the
world *all* men are sensitive to, it is their performance in
bed. And especially the first time. If a guy doesn't live up
to your last boyfriend, or your last ten lovers, or whatever
your image might be—the first time is definitely NOT the
right time to tell him. No man deliberately comes too
quickly, or enjoys needing a few minutes to reload. We're
just human.

FREE ADVICE: All the coaxing in the world can't revive
a dead horse. However, a little love and attention and
patience can make a better lover out of a first-time par-
amour. If you're thinking of this guy for the long haul,
give the sexual relationship time to grow. Men respond

better to comfort than pressure, and that usually means just a few more trial runs to really start getting it right.

"I Know You Won't Believe This, But . . ."

The setup:

Bruce and DeeDee have been dating for about three months and really like each other a lot. There has been a lot of fooling around, but still no making love. Finally, one night, DeeDee has Bruce over at her place and she's definitely in the mood to take that final step. However, Bruce seems rather nervous and hesitant.

> DEEDEE
> (Between kisses)
> Is everything okay, Bruce?

> BRUCE
> Well, yeah. Why?

He halfheartedly dives back into their making out.

> DEEDEE
> Whoa, hang on. Take it easy.

> BRUCE
> Sorry.

> DEEDEE
> No, it's nothing. I just wanted to talk a little.

> BRUCE
> Is something wrong?

DEEDEE
Well, I was actually wondering the same with you?

BRUCE
Really? Why?

DEEDEE
You just seem a little—nervous—tonight.

BRUCE
Oh, no. I don't think so.

DEEDEE
Okay. Maybe it's just me.

DeeDee attacks him with renewed vigor.

BRUCE
(Stopping her)
Well actually—

DEEDEE
What?

BRUCE
There is something I've been sort of wanting to talk to you about.

DEEDEE
Yeah?

BRUCE
(Nervously)
It's about, well, uhh this.

DEEDEE
About what?

BRUCE
This. Fooling around?

DEEDEE
(Dread in her voice)
Is there something you've got to tell me?

BRUCE
Yeah. I'm afraid there is.

DEEDEE
(Bracing herself for bad news)
Well?

BRUCE
Uhhh, ummm, I don't know how to tell you
this, but, but, I've, uhhh, never done this
before. . . .

DEEDEE
Done what?

BRUCE
Done "it." You know—

DEEDEE
(Awash in relief)
You mean you're a—

BRUCE
Yeah. You don't have to say *the* word.

DEEDEE
So you've never made love to anyone before?

                    BRUCE
                  (Ashamed)
Why don't you just broadcast it to the whole
building?

                    DEEDEE
          (Wraps her arms around him)
Bruce! I am so glad you told me.

                    BRUCE
We can still be friends, can't we?

                    DEEDEE
Are you kidding?

                    BRUCE
I mean I can understand if you don't want to.

                    DEEDEE
Have I told you what a great kisser you are?

                    BRUCE
No.

                    DEEDEE
How much I love fooling around with you?

                    BRUCE
                  (Modestly)
Well, uhhh, no . . .

                    DEEDEE
Do you *want* to make love with someone? I
mean it's not like some religious thing, is it?

                    BRUCE
Not unless being shy is a religion. And yes,

I'd like to make love with someone—with someone like you.

> DEEDEE
> (Looks him in the eye)
> Well, I'd be very excited to be your first. When you feel like you're ready. There's no rush. . . .

Bruce's Take:

He's breathing a huge sigh of relief, tinged with a heady rush of excitement. Regardless of the reason Bruce has seen every other relationship fail, DeeDee has made it clear she is willing and eager to be his first. What's more, she is patient enough to let him feel totally comfortable with both the physical and emotional aspects of this very big deal. Her kindness and understanding on sexual matters is the sort that would make any man fall in love—not just lust—with a new girlfriend.

BREAKING NEWS: There are plenty of male virgins out there. And most of them are virgins not because they have some problem, but because they are shy and fell behind the pack when their male counterparts were "strutting their stuff." If you're going through an "all-guys-are-jerks" phase, try spending time with a shy guy. Often under the quiet veneer is a terrific lover waiting to be discovered.

An Apple for the Teacher

The setup:

Barry and Rhonda have been dating for half a year and sleeping together for three months. While their relationship is strong and romantic, their sex life is definitely lacking, and they've reached a point where they both know it—though that emotion has gone totally unexpressed. They are lying in bed on a Sunday morning after a rather lame session of lovemaking the previous night.

                    RHONDA
Barry? Are you awake?

                    BARRY
Since dawn.

                    RHONDA
Me too. Is anything wrong?

                    BARRY
No. I guess not. You?

                    RHONDA
Not really. Just stuff on my mind.

                    BARRY
Yeah. Me too.

                    RHONDA
You first.

                    BARRY
No. You!

                    RHONDA
Okay. Can I ask you something?

                    BARRY
Sure.

                    RHONDA
Do you enjoy making love with me?

BARRY
Yes. A lot. I really like you.

RHONDA
I really like you, too. But I've noticed when
we make love, you don't seem to be having
such a great time?

BARRY
Funny you should mention that.

RHONDA
Is that what you were thinking about?

BARRY
Well, after last night I thought you seemed
kind of blue. I guess that's not exactly the reaction one hopes for after making love to one's
girlfriend.

RHONDA
Well, I've noticed that lately you seem to be
trying really hard when we fool around, but it
sort of seems like work, not play to you.

BARRY
I guess I can tell I'm not exactly driving you
mad with desire.

RHONDA
That's not true. I really love being with you.

BARRY
You do?

RHONDA
Yes. I do. I just think we can, how do I say
this—

BARRY
(Glumly)
Just say it.

RHONDA
I think we need to practice more!

BARRY
Practice more?

RHONDA
Yeah. There are ways . . . stuff . . . just things
I could show you that would really be fun.
For both of us!

BARRY
Am I that boring?

RHONDA
No. Not at all. Am I?

BARRY
(Surprised)
No. You totally turn me on. I think about you
all the time.

RHONDA
Really?

BARRY
Honest.

RHONDA
So would you mind if we just fooled around a
little more, a little differently. You know,
taught each other a few new tricks?

BARRY
I'm getting excited just thinking about it.

RHONDA
I noticed. Me too. Say, have you ever—

Barry's Take:

How can you not love a woman who wants to show you how to drive her to ecstasy? Patience, a sense of humor, desire, and a good relationship are all keys to great sex. But so many guys have experienced the opposite—where a woman makes them feel useless in bed. This doesn't inspire greatness. It kills desire. If sex with your lover has been falling short of late, gently broach the subject of change and exploration. Handled delicately, most guys will consider this an invite to be a kid in a candy shop— and you will be the sole beneficiary of their enthusiasm.

Body Parts

The setup:

It's a hot summer's night and Yvonne and Eric have just made love for the first time. Eric is contentedly glowing, naked on top of the rumpled sheets. Yvonne has already put her shirt back on and she's pulling the sheets over her body and rolling over, away from Eric.

ERIC
Yvonne—what are you doing?

YVONNE
(Nervously)
Going to sleep. Do you want me to leave?

ERIC
Good gosh no. I want you to come over here.

Yvonne reluctantly slides over next to Eric in the bed, dragging the sheets and blanket with her.

YVONNE
How's this?

ERIC
That's great. Are you cold?

YVONNE
No.
(Covers herself even more)
I mean, yeah.

ERIC
It's like 110 degrees in here.

YVONNE
I'm fine.

ERIC
Come on. I'm not going to bite you. You don't have to sleep in your shirt.

YVONNE
Maybe I should go.

ERIC
Hunhhh? Why?

YVONNE
(Looking for any excuse)
You'll probably be more comfortable. I don't
want to keep you up all night.

ERIC
Yvonne. I've spent three months waiting for
you to keep me up all night!

YVONNE
Really?

ERIC
Yes, really. Now take off that silly T-shirt and
come over here.

YVONNE
I'll keep it on.

ERIC
YVONNE!

YVONNE
I'm just more comfortable.

ERIC
(Scratching his chin)
May I ask a dopey question?

YVONNE
I guess so.

ERIC
We just made extraordinary love for the past
hour and a half. I've never been with a sexier
woman in my entire life. Why are you acting
like we just necked for the first time?

YVONNE

Well, I'm kind of shy.

ERIC

You didn't seem very shy back there on the dining-room table.

YVONNE

I mean shy about my body.

ERIC
(Eyes widening)
Are you joking?

YVONNE

No. Why? Do you hate it?

ERIC

Hate your body?

YVONNE

I knew it. Do you have a flannel shirt I can borrow?

ERIC

Yvonne?

YVONNE
(Unhappily)
What?

ERIC

I'll get you my long johns and a raincoat if it makes you feel more comfortable. But I want you to know something?

YVONNE

What?

ERIC

I think you have the sexiest body I have ever
seen. I want to spend like the next three weeks
just memorizing it. So if you feel shy, that's
fine. But don't feel shy on my account, because
I think you are way, way *hot!*

YVONNE

Do you really mean that?

ERIC

I promise you. I wouldn't be here if I didn't.

Eric's Take:

Having just spent three months courting Yvonne, fantasizing about Yvonne, and eagerly trying to get her into bed—
of course Eric means it when he says he loves her body.
No matter what her body looks like! Women are infinitely
harsher on themselves than guys. If we've gone to the
lengths we go to get you naked, it's because we love what
we see. Being a little timid the first few times is fine. Even
cute. But try not to hide from a man after he makes love
to you. He wouldn't have put himself in that position
unless he adored every inch of you, body included.

Chapter 6
THE RELATIONSHIP GAME

Second Fiddle

The setup:

Helen and Jake have been dating long enough that it is pretty much assumed they're going to spend both nights of the weekend together. Helen calls Jake at work at four on a Friday afternoon to talk about the weekend plans.

HELEN
(On the phone)

Hey, Jake.

JAKE
(On the phone)
Helen. I was just about to call you.

HELEN
Because you were thinking sexy things?

150

                    JAKE
Absolutely!

                    HELEN
I'm so glad. Me too. So can we talk about the
weekend?

                    JAKE
That's why I was calling!

                    HELEN
Oh good. This has been a hellacious week at
work, and I'm really tired, so I don't really
want to do too much tonight—

                    JAKE
Perfect. Because—

                    HELEN
             (Not paying attention)
—I thought we could rent a movie. You know,
something dopey and old and black and
white. Maybe a *Thin Man* movie, or *Philadel-
phia Story*. And I'm going to make you dinner
tonight at my place. You in the mood for a
nice garlicky pasta and some red wine?

                    JAKE
Uhhhh, Helen? Actually, I was calling because,
ummm, Darrell's in town tonight.

                    HELEN
Who's Darrell?

                    JAKE
One of my college buddies. I thought I told
you about him. He's pretty out of control.

HELEN
Oh really.

JAKE
Yeah. So me and Nat and Jerry were sort of planning to go out for a beer or two after work?

HELEN
Well that's okay. Can you come over after beers?

JAKE
Hmmm. Well, uhh, that might be a little late for dinner.

HELEN
Well how late?

JAKE
Well, you know, we haven't seen Darrell in a while so, ummm, dinner might not be such a hot idea. How do you feel about a nice romantic breakfast?

Long, long pause.

HELEN
Maybe I'll see you next week.

JAKE
Hey! C'mon, Helen. I just want to go out with my buddies.

HELEN
Fine. Am I stopping you?

JAKE
You don't exactly sound enthusiastic.

HELEN
Don't worry. It's no problem. I plan a romantic dinner and you blow me off to get drunk with your frat buddies. Why should I be annoyed?

JAKE
Helen, you didn't even mention this until just now.

HELEN
Ohhh. I see. Now I need to schedule my Friday nights with you in advance?

JAKE
That's not what I said. We didn't know Darrell was coming until this afternoon.

HELEN
Fine. At least I know where I fit in the pecking order.

JAKE
(After a long pause)
Okay. You're right. I'm sorry. I'll call the guys and tell them I can't make it. What do you want me to bring for dinner?

Jake's Take:

Boyish pleasures plus sincere guilt equals one unhappy boyfriend. Helen's request to see Jake was a fair one. But in a new romance, men are slow to give up certain habits—like leaving the toilet seat up, or going drinking with the guys. So what's a girl to do? In this instance, she should cut Jake a little slack. Especially if it's the first time he's sprung the old college friends routine. It's not a personal reflection on her desirability. And having made her plea, she's earned a chit for about the next month of Friday nights. Give a guy a little leash with his pals on occasion, and he will be indebted to you for a month of Fridays.

Sorry Dear, I've Got a Headache

The setup:

Rachel and Steve are in the throes of a long-term relationship that is balancing right on the precipice of the next step. They spend most of their weekends together, keep toothbrushes and underwear at each other's places, and are exclusively dating. It's a Saturday night and they're staying in, renting a movie. It happens to be a foreign film and Steve is falling sound asleep.

> RACHEL
> Honey? Honey? You're snoring.

> STEVE
> Hunghh? Oh. Sorry. Great flick.

> RACHEL
> You picked it.

> STEVE
> Yeah I did, didn't I?

> RACHEL
> We don't have to watch it. It's not that great.

She curls up on top of Steve and kisses him. He kisses her back with less than a ton of passion.

RACHEL
(Joking)
What kind of kiss is that?

STEVE
(Yawning)
A tired one?

RACHEL
So I'm no more interesting than the movie?

She kisses him again and tries to arouse her tired lover.

STEVE
(Through her kisses)
Hmm. Umm. Hey, Rach? I'm sort of exhausted tonight?

RACHEL
Maybe this will wake you up!

She tries one more time with a deep passionate kiss and a well-placed hand. Steve gently stops her.

RACHEL
(Upset now)
What's wrong?

STEVE
Nothing honey. I'm just half awake.

RACHEL
I know. I'm trying to wake up the other half!

STEVE
I know you are, but honest. I'm not really in the mood. Can we just go to bed?

RACHEL
That's exactly what I was thinking!

STEVE
I mean to sleep.

RACHEL
Well, you're a lot of fun tonight.

STEVE
Aren't I allowed to *not* be in the mood once in a while?

RACHEL
Well, I don't know. Have I gotten that boring to you?

STEVE
No. I'm just too tired to fool around.

RACHEL
(Hurt)
I don't think I've ever had a guy say that to me.

STEVE
Well, I'm not every other guy you've been with!

RACHEL
That's pretty obvious, because most guys aren't too tired to have sex on a Saturday night!

Steve's Take:

Alarm bells are going off in his head. This is the kind of conversation that leads to bad fights and ugly breakups. There are men who do not want sex every night. That happens to be a sign that you're in a long and more lasting relationship. It's comforting for a guy *not* to have to wow you with his sexual prowess. Rachel struck a low blow by comparing Steve to other lovers. And if she wants a stallion, there are plenty of guys who'd be happy to provide stud service. But if she is interested in a longer relationship, she may have to realize that in the real world, lovers sometimes take nights off—and don't necessarily want to be harassed for it.

The Ex Files

The setup:

Alan and Denise have been dating long enough that they spend every weekend together and have a truly honest and trusting relationship. No secrets necessary. It's Friday night and Alan has made Denise a nice dinner at his place. No big deal, just hanging out together enjoying one another's company to start the weekend.

> DENISE
> How was your day, hon?

> ALAN
> (Stirring the tomato sauce)
> Not bad. Glad it's Friday. You?

> DENISE
> Ughhh. Long week. Lousy day. I tried to call

you about a hundred times. You weren't answering any calls.

ALAN

I was out. Took a long lunch.

DENISE

Yeah? With who?

ALAN
(Nonchalantly)

Julia.

DENISE

Julia?

ALAN

Julia. You know, Julia?

DENISE

Julia your old girlfriend?

ALAN

Julia my buddy for six years.

DENISE

That would be the buddy you were sleeping with for five of them?

ALAN

Yes. And I'd definitely say "sleeping" was the operative word there.

DENISE

Forget it. Sorry I asked.

ALAN

Wait a second. I'm sorry you had a bad day,

but when did my friend Julia become off-limits?

DENISE

Who said anything about "off-limits." You can go out with whoever you want to.

ALAN
(Incredulous)
Go "out with"? I had lunch with her.

DENISE

I don't care if you *had* Julia for lunch on your desk. It's none of my business.

ALAN

Hello! Denise, would I be telling you I had lunch with Julia if we were having an affair?

DENISE

I don't know. Maybe.

ALAN

Denise? Denise?

DENISE
(Pouting)
What?

ALAN

I don't want to have sex with Julia.

DENISE

Really?

ALAN

If it hurts your feelings, I don't even want to have lunch with her again.

                    DENISE
            (Feeling like a jerk, now)
Don't be stupid. I'm sorry. You can have lunch
with whoever you like.

                    ALAN
And you're not going to be jealous?

                    DENISE
Well, of course I am.

                    ALAN
            (Teasing her)
Promise?

                    DENISE
Don't push your luck, buster, or else—

                    ALAN
Or else what?

                    DENISE
Or else I'm having lunch with my ex, Tommy.

                    ALAN
Who's Tommy?

                    DENISE
He was a linebacker at Maryland. About 6'4",
really cute—

Alan just makes a face at her.

Alan's Take:

In cases like this, turnabout is fair play, and Alan has no
choice but to laugh. But the truth is, we will never under-

stand how you can get so angry if we remain buds with our old girlfriend. You're still friends with *your* exes, and we usually end up meeting them and drinking beer and playing pool and inviting them to our wedding. But if *we* so much as mention an ex, you assume we want to sleep with her again. If your boyfriend is honest enough to admit he keeps in touch with an ex, you can pretty safely assume it is nothing more than a friendship.

TRUE FACT: Men do not cheat with old girlfriends. Reason? We've slept with them already. No challenge. No novelty. No reason to go there again. So, it's okay to vent if your boyfriend sees an ex occasionally, but try not to stir up a hornet's nest, because the odds are it will be one of the more worthless fights you ever get into.

Man's Failing Memory

The setup:

Mick, who has been dating June for over a year, has been out of town on a long and grueling business trip. They have a dinner date for Friday night that he is going to straight from the airport. He arrives at a fancy restaurant and finds June decked out in a sexy new dress. (He, by the way, is forty minutes late because of thunderstorms over Chicago.)

JUNE
(Gets up to kiss him)
Hey, Mickey. Welcome home. I'm so glad to see you.

MICK
Juney-June. Hi, hon. You look amazing.

JUNE
Thanks.

MICK
Wow. New dress? What's the occasion?

JUNE
You're funny.
            (She kisses him over the table)
So did you bring me something?

MICK
Uhhhhh, peanuts from the airplane?

JUNE
No, pinhead. For tonight?

MICK
Ummm tonight? What's tonight?

JUNE
You're joking, right?

MICK
Uhh, yeah. Tonight. Tonight. June, what's
tonight?

JUNE
What do you mean what's tonight? How can
you not know?

MICK
I'm starting to think tonight is—our
anniversary?

JUNE
            (Crestfallen)
You forgot.

MICK
Forgot? Of course not. It's our, uhhhhhh, anniversary of our first date? That's it.

June just stares at him.

MICK (cont'd)
Our first date was on New Year's Eve. It's July. I guess that isn't it.

JUNE
I can't believe you.

MICK
Uhhh, first kiss?

JUNE
Forget it.

MICK
No. Wait a second. You look so beautiful. It must be the first time we—Oh, sweetie. You're so special to remember.

JUNE
Get a life, Mick.

MICK
I didn't think that was it.

JUNE
Forget it. Let's just order dinner.

MICK
No. Tell me. When we first held hands? Uhh, when we were first introduced? When I first saw you naked?

JUNE
Mick. Give it a rest, will ya?

MICK
Okay. I screwed up. Are you going to tell me how?

JUNE
I'll give you a hint. If we have dessert, you might ask the waiter to put a candle in my crème brûlée. . . .

Mick's Take:

"Whoops." And credit June for not lopping his head off. You see, guys have the worst memory for special occasions. They annually forget their parents' anniversary and birthdays, their own anniversary (why do you think men like wedding bands inscribed), any conceivable anniversary with a girlfriend, and in June's case—her birthday. But June has handled the situation with great panache, and we applaud her. Please don't kill your man for an honest mistake. Chide him, remind him, and demand a very expensive retroactive gift—but punishing him will never solve the problem. June handled the situation perfectly, and we can only hope Mick will reward her justly for his own ignorance.

Brain Drain Relief

The setup:

Conrad is sitting in his office at 11 P.M. on a Thursday night, working late for the umpteenth night in a row on some long, horrible project. His girlfriend of a year, Audrey, calls. He tiredly takes her call.

> CONRAD
> (On Phone)

Hey.

> AUDREY
> (On Phone)

Hey yourself, Con. You hanging in there?

> CONRAD
> (Grumpy as all)

Barely. What's up?

> AUDREY

Nothing. Are you coming over tonight?

> CONRAD

I don't think so. I'm going to be here all night anyway.

> AUDREY

I don't care when you come over.

> CONRAD

You really want me crawling into bed at four in the morning?

> AUDREY

I want you crawling into bed any ol' time of the day or night.

> CONRAD
> (Begrudgingly)

Thanks.

AUDREY
Look, I know you're superbusy, but do we
have any plans for the weekend?

CONRAD
I may have to work.

AUDREY
(Really trying here)
I know. But I was wondering, if you brought
your laptop to my place, maybe I could set
you up in the guest room. I wouldn't get in
your way or anything, and you could use my
printer and phone and all.

CONRAD
Thanks, but it's probably better if I just do it
here. And besides, I don't want to drag you
into this nightmare I'm working on.

AUDREY
Con—you're not dragging me into anything.

CONRAD
Wouldn't you rather do something with your
friends? Or visit your sister and her kids?

AUDREY
You know what I'd like to do?

CONRAD
Find a new boyfriend? One with a better job?

AUDREY
I'd like to make you breakfast on Saturday
morning. And coffee. And proofread anything
you need help with. And make you lunch and

dinner and a midnight snack if you want
one—

CONRAD
I don't even know why you bother.

AUDREY
Because maybe in between all your work I
could rub your neck and give you a great mas-
sage—and maybe even coax you into a nice
long bath and, well, who knows what else?

CONRAD
(Can't help but smile)
You know you're crazy.

AUDREY
You know I adore you.

CONRAD
(Tapping away at his computer)
Keep the bed warm. I'll be there before the
sun comes up. . . .

Conrad's Take:

He's going to find some flowers for Audrey at the all-
night convenience store, because he considers himself one
very lucky guy. No denying it, work is a huge part of all
of our lives. It often comes with long hours and frequent
crises. When a man is moving deeply into the commitment phase of a new relationship, he looks to a woman
to see if she is a partner in life, as well as a lover. Audrey's patience and compassion will make her a prime
candidate in Conrad's heart.

The Bare Truth

The setup:

Gail and Perry have been dating comfortably for a couple of years and recently moved in together. Perry is out on a Saturday night with several of his buddies, ostensibly for a few beers and sports and whatnot. He gets home buzzed and, after attempting to tone down his beer breath, crawls into bed with Gail.

> GAIL
> Don't you smell lovely.

> PERRY
> We did a couple of tequila shots at the end of the night. I brushed twice!

> GAIL
> Don't worry about it, honey. Just don't breathe in the direction of the aquarium if you want to your fish to live.

> PERRY
> Arh har har har har!

> GAIL
> So where did you guys go?

> PERRY
> Hmm. Pete's Tavern. The Main Street Grill. And we grabbed a nightcap at Shooters.

> GAIL
> Shooters? Isn't that a lap-dancing club?

PERRY

Yeah. Why?

GAIL

Someone getting married tomorrow?

PERRY

No.

GAIL

So if this wasn't a bachelor's party, what were
you doing at a lap-dancing club?

PERRY
(Innocently)
Watching girls take their clothes off?

GAIL

I can't believe you!

PERRY

Why? What did I do?

GAIL

You actually went to a strip club while I sat
home talking to my mom on the phone all
night?

PERRY

Hey, if I had known you were talking to your
mom—

GAIL
(Really upset)
I'm not joking!

PERRY

You know, Gail, it wasn't like some big deal.
None of us even got our own lap-dance.

GAIL

Ooooh! You should have told me. That makes
it just dandy.

PERRY

Hey, you know, I thought maybe I'd score
some brownie points here for being honest?
Would you rather I lied about where we
went?

GAIL

Yeah. If you and your juvenile-delinquent
friends insist on going to strip clubs, maybe I
would!

Perry's Take:

He is caught off guard by Gail's outrage. You see, Perry
thought he and Gail had the kind of relationship where
he could tell her anything. Even the fact that he went to
a strip joint. What is she saying now—don't go, or lie to
me when you do? This puts us in a quandary. Lying
seems a much greater sin than watching a couple of strip-
pers dance for an hour. Before you accost your boyfriend,
consider this: if he is truthful about one bawdy evening,
then you probably have nothing to worry about. If he lies
about it, then what else might he start lying about? Probably better to forgive him his sins, as long as it doesn't
become a habit.

TRUE CONFESSION: Strip clubs are really pretty boring.
The expectation is much greater than the reality. If the
truth be known, guys usually stay for about three dances

until the girls all start to look the same. Then they bail out and find a bar where the beers are cheaper and they can watch a game and talk.

Dinner with Your Folks, Again?

The setup:

Tim and Charlotte have been dating for about five months and the relationship is reasonably serious; they're happy together. However, Charlotte's parents, whom Tim has met several times, are obsessed with their daughter getting married. It's Saturday morning, and Tim and Charlotte are just waking up together at her place after a nice Friday night date. The phone rings.

> CHARLOTTE (ON PHONE)
> Hello? Oh, hey, Mom. What's up?
> (Pause)
> Not much. Just hanging out with Tim.
> (Pause)
> Tonight? No. No big plans, I don't think so.
>   (She looks at Tim who is frantically
>   waving "NO")
> Sure. We'd be happy to come over for dinner.
> Eight okay? Great. See you then.

Charlotte hangs up the phone.

> TIM
> Why did you do that?

> CHARLOTTE
> Do what? Did we have plans for tonight?

                    TIM
We might have.

                    CHARLOTTE
You just said five minutes ago, ''Let's stay in
tonight and rent a video or something.''

                    TIM
I know. That's a plan!

                    CHARLOTTE
Oh sure. Hey, Ma, we can't come over because
Tim hasn't seen *Terminator III* yet?

                    TIM
Maybe I just wanted to hang out with you
alone.

                    CHARLOTTE
That's sweet, honey. We can hang out alone—
after we have dinner with Mom and Dad.

                    TIM
                (Dejectedly)
What happened to my vote in our weekend
plans?

                    CHARLOTTE
Do you have a problem with my parents?

                    TIM
Well, no. They're very nice. Usually.

                    CHARLOTTE
What's *that* supposed to mean?

                    TIM
Nothing. I'm sorry.

CHARLOTTE

No, don't back out on that one. What did you mean?

TIM

Well, it's just that, well, they can be a little overbearing sometimes.

CHARLOTTE

I can't believe you said that. They're absolutely wonderful to you.

TIM

I know. They are. But they can be a bit much, especially when they go into that "cornering" routine?

CHARLOTTE

What are you talking about?

TIM

You know, your mother sweetly calls you into the kitchen to wash the artichokes or something—and your dad grills me about my intentions?

CHARLOTTE

He does not!

TIM

(Imitates her dad)
"So, Tim, if you make VP this year, do you think you'll be buying a house soon? You know this neighborhood has a lot of good values in three and four bedrooms—that is, if you think you're going to start a family. . . ."

                    CHARLOTTE
You're exaggerating.

                    TIM
Or how about your mom? "So, Tim, you know
Char is going to be thirty this year. Any
thoughts on what you're going to get her?"
Wink, wink, wink!

                    CHARLOTTE
You're being totally unfair.

                    TIM
I'm being truthful. They're wonderful people,
but do you think you can try *not* to leave me
alone with one or the other?

                    CHARLOTTE
                 (Picks up the phone)
Fine! No problem!

                    TIM
What are you doing?

                    CHARLOTTE
Calling Mom back to cancel. Obviously you
don't want to spend time with them. . . .

Tim's Take:

"Oh boy, how did I get myself into this mess?!!" Little-
known medical fact: Guys are born with their feet in their
mouths. Tim may not have broached this subject delicately, but on the other hand, men do not respond well
to pushy potential in-laws, especially if you've only been
dating a few months. If Charlotte's parents are truly ridiculous, then she needs to ask Tim nicely to humor them.

Or have a talk with her folks and beg them to back off.
No man in history has jacked up the speed of a relationship because his girlfriend's mother wants to pick out
china patterns.

Living with Pigpen

The setup:

Susan has been dating Joe for almost a year and they
spend plenty of weekends together at each other's apartments. On this Friday night Susan comes back to Joe's
and stays over. She gets up the next morning before Joe
to make some coffee and is somewhat dismayed to find
the apartment one step short of being condemned.

> SUSAN
> (Nudging Joe awake)
> Are you up?

> JOE
> Yeah. Sort of. Morning.

> SUSAN
> You want some coffee?

> JOE
> Sure. I'll have a sip. You're up early.

> SUSAN
> Yeah. Just thinking about the day. Do we have
> any plans?

> JOE
> Keep sleeping?

SUSAN
You're incorrigible.

JOE
Nope. Just tired. What do you want to do?

SUSAN
I don't know. It's a nice rainy day. How about
we do some house projects?

JOE
House projects? Like what?

SUSAN
I don't know. Just something kind of fun and
stay home-y . . . hang out together.

JOE
Hey. I have a good idea. My old electric trains
are in the attic. Wanna set them up today?

SUSAN
(Rolling her eyes)
I was thinking more along the lines of tearing
things down, not setting them up.

JOE
(Getting it)
Ahhhhh. Little trouble finding a coffee cup this
morning?

SUSAN
(Running with the cue)
Joe—your kitchen is a disaster area. There are
dirty dishes from the birthday dinner I made
you—last month!

JOE

They're still soaking.

SUSAN

Even the roaches won't go in that water.

JOE

I'll straighten up later, I promise. Why don't you come back to bed and snuggle up and enjoy the rain.

SUSAN
(Very awake)

Why don't you go back to sleep—and I'll go out and get some stuff for breakfast.

JOE

And?

SUSAN

And what?

JOE

And what else have you got up your sleeve?

SUSAN
(Innocently)

I thought maybe I'd pick up a thing or two at the store. Have you ever heard of—Fantastik?

JOE

Why don't we do this tomorrow?

SUSAN

How about if I bribe you?

JOE

What did you have in mind?

SUSAN

I'll get fresh bagels and lox from your favorite deli—if you'll at least look remotely interested in making this place habitable.

JOE

How about if we skip the cleaning and just fool around all morning?

SUSAN

What if I get the bagels and lox, and we clean up enough to set the electric trains up?

JOE
(Sits up in bed)

The trains?

SUSAN

And we can fool around, *if* you'll help me clean your bathroom!

JOE
(Kissing her)

Deal!

Joe's Take:

Sex, breakfast, *and* he gets to play with his trains from boyhood—all for just agreeing to help straighten out his house? This sounds like a terrific deal, and Susan gets all the credit because she was so good-natured. Guys who live like slobs can't help it. If you fight them, they'll just hide all the dirty laundry somewhere you can't find it— until it starts to reproduce. However, if you're really nice about it—and make cleaning feel like part of being together as a couple—we tend to melt like butter. Feels sort of grown-up, which is always a good sign for a growing relationship.

Chapter 7
WEEKENDS THAT LAST FOREVER

Knowing When to Say No

The setup:

Marcia and Brian have been dating for about a month, and while they've fooled around pretty extensively, they've not yet slept together. They've not even spent a night together. Brian calls Marcia on a Wednesday afternoon to ask her out.

> BRIAN
> Marcia, it's Brian.

> MARCIA
> Hi. How you doing?

> BRIAN
> I'm great. You?

MARCIA
Good thanks. What's up?

BRIAN
Well . . . I was thinking—are you busy this weekend?

MARCIA
I'm not sure. Which night?

BRIAN
Both!

MARCIA
Hmmm. I don't know. Why?

BRIAN
Well, I've got some frequent-flyer mileage I need to use up, and there's this really great B&B I know in Bermuda. Do you like the beach?

MARCIA
I love the beach.

BRIAN
Really! Me too. So you up for a weekend in Bermuda?

MARCIA
Gee, I don't know, Brian. You know, we've only been on a couple of dates. I don't usually make a habit of just hopping on a plane with guys—

BRIAN
This place is right on a cove. Got a great fire-

place in the room. Warm days, cool nights.
You ever seen the pink beaches in Bermuda?

MARCIA
I've heard they're gorgeous.

BRIAN
So what do you say—a little adventure could
be fun?

MARCIA
I agree. And I'd love to. How about we make
a deal.

BRIAN
(Hopeful)
Talk to me.

MARCIA
I'll take a rain check on the adventure, if you
let me make you dinner at my place Saturday
night. Special dinner!

BRIAN
Your place?

MARCIA
I'll toss my roommate out. It's my party. You
bring the wine?

BRIAN
So rain check on the Bermuda, hunghh?

MARCIA
Absolutely. Bermuda's not going
anywhere. . . . Are you in?

Brian's Take:

You bet Brian's in. Why? Because Marcia offered an appealing alternative to his invite. She may like this guy, and she may be attracted to him, but why risk spoiling the whole affair before it's even gotten out of the gate. If a man asks you away for the weekend, you can bank on the fact he'll be looking for sex two minutes after you hit the hotel. You may want that, too, but why not explore those feelings on more familiar ground. By inviting Brian to her place, she alluded to the fact that good things may be coming soon. It's a surefire way to win Brian's attention. He'll be looking forward to Saturday night—and Bermuda will be a lot more fun after they've tested the waters back home.

Country Comfort?

The setup:

Lois, an advertising executive, is a thirty-year-old city girl. Trent, a coworker, is a bearded, ponytailed creative person at the agency. They have been dating for six weeks and occasionally spending nights together. They are away on their first weekend date, and Trent has mapped out a wilderness camping trip—where he happens to be the wilderness guide. They've hiked all day and spent the night in a tent. It's daybreak the next morning—the time when all good campers arise—and Trent is up and out of the tent.

TRENT
(Calls into the tent)
Morning. You want coffee, Lois?

LOIS
Ohhh God. I want a shower and a hard bed.

> TRENT
>
> C'mon out. It's a glorious day.

> LOIS
>
> I'm not coming out of this sleeping bag until the temperature gets above freezing.

> TRENT
>
> C'mon, Lois. It's just a little chilly. I've got the fire going.

Lois, looking absolutely depleted, pokes her head out of the tent.

> LOIS
>
> I think I heard bears last night.

> TRENT
>
> I haven't seen a bear up here in ten years.

> LOIS
>
> Then maybe it was snakes. Growling snakes.

> TRENT
> (Making light of the situation)
> There might have been a squirrel rustling around. What do you want with your coffee?

> LOIS
>
> Room service! Some smoked salmon, a poppy bagel. Fresh squeezed OJ?

> TRENT
>
> I've got some nice bran trail mix and dehydrated milk.

> LOIS
> That sounds—crunchy!

TRENT
(Sucks in the fresh morning air)
Isn't this fabulous?

LOIS
Trent?

TRENT
Yeah? Is something wrong?

LOIS
I don't know how to tell you this, but, ummm,
I don't think this is so fabulous.

TRENT
Oh, come on. You just got to get up and get
the blood circulating.

LOIS
No, I need to get up and have a hot shower,
maybe some breakfast in bed, and a day at the
spa!

TRENT
But you said you wanted to try camping.

LOIS
I said it sounds fun—in theory.

TRENT
Hey, we're here. It's going to warm up soon
and be a beautiful day. There's a nice gentle
hike to the summit of Bluebonnet Mountain.

LOIS
Trent! I want to take a nice gentle hike to my
doormanned apartment. Would that be okay?

Trent's Take:

Uh oh! Big miscalculation on his part. Better to bail and save face at this stage of the game. But in all fairness, half the blame for the weekend lies with Lois as well. Weekends with new mates are not the time to take soul-searching expeditions. If you're not sure about this camping thing, suggest an in-between. Maybe a stay at a bed-and-breakfast with an easy day hike nearby. Trent should have been more specific warning Lois what she was in for. But Lois probably could have guessed this weekend was not for her in the first place—and said something in advance.

FREE ADVICE: Sleeping outdoors is definitely not for everyone. If a man invites you on a weekend that doesn't strike you as wildly romantic, the chances are it is wildly the opposite. Tell him your concerns and plan something else. If he's insistent on camping or motocross or deer hunting, best you bag the weekend, and perhaps him as well. Your interests may be too far apart to make the romance fly.

Kidnapped!

The setup:

Brad is sitting in his office on a Friday afternoon scribbling down notes and talking to his new girlfriend of two months, Teri. He's doing a lot more listening than talking, and smiling all the way.

> BRAD
> (On the phone)
> Wait. Hello? Teri. Slow down. You're picking
> me up at what time?

TERI
(Also on the phone)
Seven in the morning. Can you handle that?

BRAD
Well, yeah. But why don't you just stay over
and we can leave together?

TERI
Because this is my surprise. My treat. Can I
make these plans please?

BRAD
Anything you say, boss. So what should I
bring?

TERI
Well, let's see. A sports coat. No tie. A couple
of tennis shirts and a T-shirt. Hiking boots. A
swimsuit. Umm, your tennis racket—

BRAD
C'mon Teri. . . . Where are we going?

TERI
I'm not telling.

BRAD
Can I ask how many nights?

TERI
Nope.

BRAD
Are you going to tell me anything?

TERI
Don't skimp on the condoms!

BRAD
(Clearing his throat)
Excuse me, dear?

TERI
I think you'll find this spot—how shall I say,
inspiring?

BRAD
(Laughing)
I'm inspired already!

TERI
Good. . . . Save your energy, cowboy. I have a
few new goodies to show you.

BRAD
Just when I thought I knew ya—

TERI
You ain't seen nothing yet. Tomorrow at
seven?

BRAD
I'll be out front at four!

Brad's Take:

This is one fun girl—the kind guys love to date. And
frankly, this scenario happens to so few guys that we wish
it would happen more often. Men feel like they always
have to make the plans. We do the asking, we usually
make the first moves, we're often expected to come up
with a good time during the courtship phase. By taking
the lead, Teri has a blank slate to have a great time with
her new boyfriend, and Brad is so excited by the unknown
that this weekend is fraught with promise. Any guy

would look forward to a mystery weekend with the kind of girl who keeps him on his toes.

Wrong Read

The setup:

Alyssa's been dating Kevin for about six weeks. While they've fooled around quite a bit, they've never slept together and never spent the night together. Kevin invites Alyssa to the wine country for an overnight date, and she readily agrees, being a great lover of wines. They've just arrived at the inn.

> KEVIN
> (Room key in hand)
> This looks like our place.

He opens the door for Alyssa and lets her in, carrying their bags behind. He closes the door behind them.

> ALYSSA
> (A dark look on her face)
> There's only one bed in here.

> KEVIN
> Uhhh, yeah. I guess there is.

> ALYSSA
> You knew that.

> KEVIN
> Knew what?

ALYSSA

Give me a break, Kevin. You deliberately
booked a room with one bed.

KEVIN

Well, no, not exactly. I did ask for a nice
room.

ALYSSA

Good. It's very nice. Now why don't you ask
for a nice cot. That is, unless you like sleeping
on the couch!

KEVIN

Hey, whoa. Hold the phone. What's wrong,
Alyssa?

ALYSSA

What do you mean what's wrong? I know
why you got me up here.

KEVIN

To ride bikes and take walks and taste wines?

ALYSSA

Very funny.

KEVIN

I'm serious!

ALYSSA

If I had known you were just trying to get me
into bed—

KEVIN

Alyssa! That's not why I brought you here. I
just wanted us to have a nice weekend
together.

ALYSSA
Why do you guys always assume a "nice
weekend" means sleeping together?

KEVIN
Well gee, I mean, I didn't assume that. But
you know, it isn't like we haven't fooled
around or anything. It wouldn't be the worst
thing in the world.

ALYSSA
See! I knew it. You brought me up here to get
me in bed. My friends all told me. I should
have known better. . . .

Kevin's Take:

Heck, yeah, she should have known better. Of course Kevin
brought Alyssa up to a beautiful B&B in the wine country
with the desire to sleep with her. That's exactly what a guy
means when he says, "Would you like to go away with
me?" This is not some subliminal message. It's a direct invite
to share a bed. You have the option to say either "No," or,
"Can we get separate rooms?" (or at least a room with two
beds). Spare everyone the embarrassment and discomfort
Kevin and Alyssa are going through. Don't accept a man's
invite to spend the weekend together unless you are willing
to consider sharing a bed with him.

A Fish Out of Water

The setup:

Duane and Theresa have been dating for two months, and

they've made love and spent nights together at one another's apartments. However, they've never ventured away for the weekend together. Duane proposes a nice little getaway by the sea at a town known both for its local artists and its local fishing. Theresa, a great lover of the sea and painting, agrees. Once there, though, she finds herself not at a gallery, but instead, in a nine-foot fishing skiff in three-foot swells.

> DUANE
> (Baiting a hook)
> Here, Theresa, watch! You slip the hook right through one end of the worm—like that—then push it through the thick part of its body—like that.

> THERESA
> (Totally grossed out)
> It's still alive! How can you do that?

> DUANE
> Well, you want it alive. You want it squirming at the end of the hook. That's what attracts the fish.

> THERESA
> (Gamely tries baiting her hook)
> Ughhhh. I can't do this. Here—

> DUANE
> That's okay. Here. Hold my rod. Whoa, big swell. Hang on. There you go. Just let the line out. . . . Say, you want a sandwich?

> THERESA
> No thank you.

DUANE
We've got salami and cheese, and smoked tur-
key with arugula.

THERESA
Actually, Duane—

DUANE
Hey. Look. You got one.

THERESA
Oh no. Here. You take it.

DUANE
No, reel it in. C'mon. It's yours!

Theresa reels and reels and reels and pulls in a big, slap-
ping, smelly flounder.

THERESA
Oh my gosh. Look at him—

DUANE
Yeah, he's a beaut!

THERESA
What are you doing?

DUANE
(Smacking the fish on the gunwale)
Stunning him so I can get the hook out.

THERESA
Duane. Can you just let him go? Please?

DUANE
Why? He's a five-pounder.

THERESA

Because, well, I can't bear watching you kill a live animal.

DUANE

Oh. You didn't tell me. Well, let me see if I can get this hook out without—whoops.

THERESA

(Eyes covered by her hands)

What happened?

DUANE

I'm sorry. His guts sort of came out with the hook. You hooked him real good.

THERESA

Uhh, look, Duane—can I tell you something?

DUANE

Sure.

THERESA

I—think—I'm—going—to—yak!

DUANE

Theresa! Do you get seasick?

THERESA

Terribly.

DUANE

Why didn't you tell me?

THERESA

You seemed so excited to go fishing.

DUANE

I thought you were, too. You said you really
wanted to come here!

THERESA
(Crestfallen)

I did. To see the local painters and the galler-
ies and the town.

DUANE

Oh.

THERESA

Do you hate me?

DUANE

Well, no. Of course not. I just wish I'd known.
Do you want to go in? We can do something
else.

THERESA
(Green around the gills)

Please?

Duane's Take:

At this particular moment he is hoping Theresa doesn't
puke and wishing she had told him about her seasickness
three hours ago. Nice guys will trip over themselves to
please you. We want you to be happy and in love and
lust and all those good things on our first weekend away.
But please, please tell us important things we need to
know before you agree to go on a date. Fear of heights?
We'll skip the rock climbing. Fair skin? We don't have to
plan an eight-hour beach day. Don't be bashful about
your wants and desires on our first trip together. It's no

fun planning a great weekend if we're not going to enjoy it together.

Jet-Lagged

The setup:

Joanne and Woody have been dating long distance for nearly a year. Long enough distance that they can't drive to see one another. Woody surprises Joanne by deciding to fly out for an unexpected visit, but oddly enough, the weekend doesn't turn out nearly as well as usual. It's Sunday night and they are both starting to get the Monday morning blues, already.

> JOANNE
> Is everything okay, Woody? You seem sort of down this weekend?

> WOODY
> Yeah. Everything's fine.

> JOANNE
> Then why do I get the feeling something's wrong?

> WOODY
> I don't know. Is something wrong?

> JOANNE
> Not with me. Is something wrong with you?

> WOODY
> No. I mean, I don't think so.

JOANNE

So since you came out this weekend, are you still planning to come out *next* weekend?

WOODY

I sort of wanted to talk to you about that.

JOANNE

So something *is* wrong.

WOODY

Well you just said you don't want to see me next weekend!

JOANNE

No. I asked if you were coming to see me *again*, next weekend.

WOODY

Well, you know, maybe we've been seeing a little too much of one another.

JOANNE

What are you talking about? We see each other, like, once a month usually.

WOODY

I know. But all the phone calls and the huge bills and then the airfares and all—it seems like we're always planning for the weekend.

JOANNE

What's wrong with that? We hardly ever see each other.

WOODY

Well, then maybe we need to start seeing other people.

JOANNE
(After a long pause)
You're already seeing someone, aren't you?

WOODY
No. Are you?

JOANNE
Of course not. Why would I want to see someone else?

WOODY
Well, don't you think this long-distance thing is wearing sort of thin?

JOANNE
I don't think so. Do you?

Woody's Take:

Apparently long distance is wearing thin for him! Otherwise, he would not have brought it up in the first place. Long distance takes its toll on couples, and in the case of guys, it can easily put them off the relationship. Too much time alone, and too much time to consider dating other women. There should be a statute of limitations: if a guy doesn't try to close the distance gap within a year, women should automatically break up with that guy for six months and see if absence makes his heart grow fonder. Otherwise, all those frequent-flyer miles may be for naught.

FREE ADVICE: If you're in a long-distance relationship, no matter how frequently you call him, cut that number in half. Make him miss you. Make him want you. It really puts the relationship to the test, and it also does wonders for the sex life. And if it doesn't, something's wrong. Time to bail!

Win, Lose, or Drawer

The setup:

Pamela and Martin have been dating for six months. They see each other at least once a week, and they usually spend the weekend together at Martin's because he doesn't have a roommate. It's a Thursday morning, and they've just spent the night after a casual weeknight date. Pamela is getting dressed in the same clothes she wore to work the day before, and it's too late for her to go home and change.

> PAMELA
> (Rummaging through a large
> handbag)
> I know I stuck a clean pair of panties and bra in here somewhere.

> MARTIN
> (Coming out of the shower)
> Hunghh?

> PAMELA
> Nothing. I feel like a tramp carrying my under-wear around in my bag.

> MARTIN
> So just don't wear any.

> PAMELA
> You'd like that.

                          MARTIN
          Well actually—

                          PAMELA
                          (Smiling)
          Forget it. Sorry I said anything.

She finds her clean undies and starts getting dressed.

                          PAMELA (Cont'd)
          Say, Martin?

                          MARTIN
          Say yeah!

                          PAMELA
          How would you feel if I borrowed one of your
          drawers?

                          MARTIN
          Borrow one of my drawers? Like to carry
          something in? I don't have time to empty out
          a drawer right now. Why don't you just use
          my laundry bag?

                          PAMELA
          No, dummy. I mean like borrow, as in keep a
          drawer for myself in your dresser?

                          MARTIN
          Why?

He truly is clueless.

                          PAMELA
          Well, like to keep a couple of clean pairs of
          panties and bras in?

Martin stares at her like she just announced she's having a sex-change operation.

> MARTIN
> Why do you need a drawer? You can carry underwear in that tote bag of yours.

> PAMELA
> You mean with my daytimer and purse and car keys and checkbook and papers?

> MARTIN
> Sure. Why not. That bag's big enough to carry a roast turkey!

> PAMELA
> That's not the point.

> MARTIN
> So what is the point?

> PAMELA
> Well, we spend like three nights a week together. It just seems stupid for me to have to schlep underwear around in my bag all week. If I had a drawer in your dresser, I wouldn't always have to run home for clean clothes.

> MARTIN
> So you want me to spend more nights at your place?

> PAMELA
> No! You know my roommate's always there. That's not the point either.

> MARTIN
> Then what *is* the point?

Pamela rolls her eyes in disgust and disappears into the bathroom.

Martin's Take:

Pam's not making herself clear about what she really wants, but Martin is being really obtuse! Obviously he is not ready to have Pamela's *underwear* move in, because that really signals the end of single life. But Pam is also at fault because she is trying to sideslip her way into something that is a lot more serious than just having clean undies. Better she ask straight out how Martin would feel if she kept some stuff at his place on a more *permanent* basis? That puts him on the spot, but this is important. It should be dealt with head-on. If Pam asks him point-blank, it gives Martin a chance to sleep on her request and then, hopefully, realize that Pam's undies in his drawers would be a good thing for both of them.

Burning the Home Fires

The setup:

Caroline and Will have been voraciously dating one another for about three months. A real lust-at-first-sight relationship full of all-night dates and weekend road trips and quirky, fun, outrageous times together. It's Friday night and Caroline has a different plan. She calls Will at work.

CAROLINE
(On phone)
Hey, Will. How you doing?

                    WILL
                (On phone)
Good. Can't wait to see you.

                  CAROLINE
Me neither.

                    WILL
Meet you at six-thirty for beers?

                  CAROLINE
Well, actually, I was thinking—

                    WILL
              (Doesn't hear her)
Let's make it six, because there's a free jazz
concert down at the Seaport. Then there's an
art opening in SoHo I wanted to check out.
After that I've picked out three places we
might go for dinner. But we've got to be done
by eleven, because there's a party uptown I
thought we'd stop by—

                  CAROLINE
Will. Hello. Will? Hold the phone—

                    WILL
What's up?

                  CAROLINE
All that stuff sounds great. But I have a
question.

                    WILL
Yeah?

                  CAROLINE
Will the world end if we miss any of it?

                    WILL
What do you mean?

                  CAROLINE
Well, I was sort of wondering—how would
you feel about spending the whole weekend
with me?

                    WILL
Well, I'd love to. Do we have plans?

                  CAROLINE
              (Thinks about this)
Uhhhh, sort of. Do you need to know them?

                    WILL
Well, I guess not. Is everything okay? Are you
angry at me?

                  CAROLINE
No! I'm crazy about you. I just want to—slow
down a little? Spend a little time together, just
you and me?

                    WILL
              (Thinks about this)
Hey. That sounds like a really neat idea.

                  CAROLINE
So can I plan this weekend?

                    WILL
I'm all yours.

                  CAROLINE
How exciting. I'm getting goose bumps!

                    WILL
So where should we meet?

                    CAROLINE
Let me see. . . . Could I interest you in dinner
at my place tonight?

                    WILL
Well yeah. What can I bring?

                    CAROLINE
Your smile and an open mind?

                    WILL
                (Laughing)
Be there in ten minutes. Don't worry about
food. . . .

Will's Take:

He's pumped! A whole weekend where he doesn't have
to impress Caroline with his encyclopedic knowledge of
the city. When we are first in a romance with you, we
have a tendency to overplan every step of the way. We
want you to be amused, fed, happy, laughing, and sexu-
ally satisfied for every second you're with us. That's what
makes us a bit overeager at times. So when you take the
weekend into your own hands, you're not only slowing
us down (mercifully in some cases), but also making a
statement of your own: you like us and you want to make
a future of it.

Visiting the Parental Units

The setup:

Delia has been dating Jim for almost a year and they are really getting serious about each other. So much so that Jim decides to bring Delia to Maine to meet his parents— a weekend "roll out the new girlfriend" trip. It is the first night of the visit and dinner is over. Delia is in the kitchen helping Jim's mom clean up. Jim is about to walk in when he overhears their voices and eavesdrops.

> JIM'S MOM
> . . . So on our first date, his father was so nervous he could barely hand the change over for the movie tickets. I guess he'd had his eye on me for a while. I thought he was going to choke over dinner. He didn't call me after that for three weeks.

> DELIA
> How come?

> MOM
> Well he said he was shy. But actually, I think he was terrified.

> DELIA
> You don't seem like the "terrifying" type.

> MOM
> No. I didn't think so either. But you know men.

> DELIA
> Don't I. Your son was very cute about asking me out the first time.

MOM
Really?

DELIA
Well he just snooped around my desk at work
for about six months. I liked him the day I
met him, and I dropped about a million hints.
He was a little slow to take the hint.

MOM
Like father like son, I guess.

DELIA
Yeah. They both have that cute crook to their
smiles.

MOM
(Thinks about this)
They do, don't they?

Finally, Jim walks in on his mom and girlfriend.

JIM
What are you guys conspiring about?

DELIA
I'll never tell.

MOM
We're thinking about taking a walk down by
the ocean.

JIM
That sounds great.

MOM
Who said anything about you.

JIM
Well thanks a lot.

MOM
Maybe we girls would like to have a little quality time together. Why don't you finish the dishes with your dad.

JIM
Great! Just what I had in mind.

DELIA
(Laughing)
That'll be a first!

JIM
(Raising an eyebrow in jest)
Am I safe leaving you two alone?

MOM
What do you think I'll do—tell embarrassing stories about you as a little boy?

DELIA
Promise?

JIM
Oh boy. What have I gotten myself into?

DELIA
I won't ask her about any of your old girlfriends. . . .

MOM
Believe me, none were as nice as you, Delia.

DELIA
(Beaming)
I like your mom, Jim. . . .

JIM
She does have impeccable taste. . . .

Jim's Take:

The fact that Delia and his mom are getting along so famously is great news—for everyone! Mom's happy. Delia's comfortable. And Jim is thrilled he can leave his honey with his mother. Men love it when you get along with their folks. If we've taken the step of bringing you home to meet the family, it means we have really serious intentions. To see you hit it off confirms our belief that you are as wonderful as we thought—and if Mom concurs, this romance may well be leading somewhere.

FREE ADVICE: If he introduces you to his best friend within a month of dating, you're in for a really fun relationship fraught with potential. If he introduces you to his parents within a month of dating, this guy is *way* serious. Don't be surprised at anything that happens from that point on.

Chapter 8
LIFELONG CONVERSATIONS

The Unspoken Truth

The setup:

Patti is sitting in her office fuming to a friend about her rotten, two-timing, no-good, soon-to-be-ex-boyfriend Keith—who has not phoned her in two days. And it's Friday night! Patti is thumbing through her Rolodex trying to decide which old flame would happily leap if she called, when the phone rings.

PATTI
(On phone)
Hello? Keith, . . . what do *you* want?

KEITH
(On phone)
Excuse me? What kind of hello is that?

PATTI
It's called the "I don't have time to talk to you" hello.

And with that, she hangs up. A second later the phone rings.

PATTI
What?

KEITH
I want to know what's wrong?

PATTI
Oh you do? Why don't you try figuring it out, Mister Smart Guy?

KEITH
It's not your birthday. . . . It's not Valentine's Day. . . . Is it some sort of anniversary? That's it! Have we been dating six months today?

PATTI
Drop dead, Keith. There are plenty of other guys who would be happy to take me out.

KEITH
I'd be happy to take you out. As a matter of fact—

PATTI
(Interrupting)
Oh I'm sure. Nothing better to do with your time I suppose?

KEITH
(Dumbfounded)
What have I done wrong here?

PATTI
(Losing her temper)
Listen, hotshot. Maybe all your old girlfriends just come when you click your fingers. But I'm not your old girlfriends! You can't just call me at four o'clock on a Friday afternoon.

KEITH
Just call you? I thought we had a date?

PATTI
(More tentatively)
We do?

KEITH
Don't we?

PATTI
Did you leave me voice mail? A message at home?

KEITH
No. I just got the tickets twenty minutes ago.

PATTI
Tickets to what?

KEITH
Courtside seats for the Lakers! A client can't use them.

PATTI
So we *didn't* have a date. Well screw you, hotshot. Take someone else.

KEITH
Patti . . . Patti! I assumed we were going to hang out this weekend!

PATTI

You did?

KEITH

Well, hell, yeah. We did last weekend. And
the weekend before. Not to mention Tuesday
night. And Wednesday morning. You haven't
forgotten Wednesday morning, have you?

PATTI
(Softens like melting ice cream)
No, I haven't forgotten Wednesday
morning. . . . But why didn't you call me to
make a date?

KEITH

Did I have to? I just assumed . . . well, gosh.
I'm sorry. I guess, well. Maybe you're seeing
someone else or something. What a dope I am.
I'm sorry. I should have—

PATTI

Keith? Keith?

KEITH

What?

PATTI

Did you really assume we were going to see
each other tonight?

KEITH

Honest!

PATTI

How come?

KEITH
Well. I don't know. Just because?

Patti smiles softly. Crisis averted.

Keith's Take:

He nearly blew it here because he crossed a boundary without holding Patti's hand. Men can be rather dense in the commitment department. We're not big on stating the obvious, so we try to just ease into that new plateau where you don't need to "make a date." It is just assumed. Of course Patti might have been a little more understanding before she blew her lid, but at least they sorted things out. And everyone knows, a good argument is a great precursor to awesome sex, so Keith and Patti's weekend is looking positively delightful!

Cliff Diving for Love

The setup:

Carrie, a woman in her thirties is dating Patrick, a man of twenty-four. Carrie is an investment banker with a solid job on the promotion track. She's been there six years. Patrick graduated from photography school a year ago and is shooting photos for the small-town gazette. While the sparks are hot and heavy between Patrick and Carrie, many of the practical aspects of their relationship are less than stellar. Patrick, who is perennially poor, invites Carrie out for a burrito.

PATRICK
(Hands Carrie the paper menu with a
flair)
Carrie—have anything you want. We're celebrating tonight.

CARRIE
(Smiling)
Anything? Burrito with "the works"?

PATRICK
Money's no object anymore. I have great news.

CARRIE
Tell, tell.

PATRICK
I have thrown the shackles of small-town jour-
nalism. I got a real job offer today.

CARRIE
That's great. Doing what?

PATRICK
A three-month photo shoot for *World View
Magazine*.

CARRIE
Wow. What are you going to be shooting?

PATRICK
India!

CARRIE
India?

PATRICK
That's right. A profile of the towns and villages of India. And they're paying me great!

CARRIE
(A little less enthusiastic)
Really? How much?

PATRICK
Four hundred dollars a week plus expenses.

CARRIE
(Droops even more)
Oh. That's wonderful.

PATRICK
So are you in?

CARRIE
Hunghh?

PATRICK
I want you to come with me.

CARRIE
To India?

PATRICK
Yeah! We'll backpack and take the third-class train all over the place to save money. We're going to see the real world. Real poverty. Real people. And we'll eat real Indian food.

CARRIE
And get real dysentery.

PATRICK
I know. It's part of the adventure.

CARRIE

Patrick—I can't quit my job and travel around India.

PATRICK

Why not? This assignment could lead to anything. Timbuktu. Casablanca. Vietnam. Bosnia. We can make love on all seven continents. I want you to be with me, Carrie.

CARRIE

I know you do. And I want to be with you. But I don't see myself abandoning my career and traveling around the world right now.

PATRICK
(The first pangs of hurt)
Why not?

CARRIE

Because . . . because, we're at different stages of our lives!

Patrick's Take:

What is Carrie talking about? Life is for living, and she should drop everything and see the sights of India with him. Patrick is clearly crazy about Carrie and crazy about life. Why should he slow down? You can't help but admire a young artist's passion, but if long-term commitment is what Carrie seeks, she needs to ask what *she's* willing to give up while Patrick chases his dreams.

YOUNG MAN WARNING: While there are obvious advantages to dating men in their early twenties (remember sex four times a night?), there is also a huge downside. Adventurous young guys like to lead adventurous young lives, sometimes blind to the responsibilities that come with age. If photo safaris and touring with rock bands and backpacking around Europe are what your love life needs, sign up. But if you are looking for more of a long-term relationship, better stock up on patience. The Patricks of the world do not settle down easily.

Drive-By Meeting

The setup:

Joel and Roberta, who have been going out for three months, have just spent a great day's outing at the beach. Their relationship has grown cozy and comfortable like an old work shirt and their romance definitely has "legs." However, neither has met a single member of the other's family. As they're driving along singing to an oldies station, Joel suddenly pulls off the highway at an exit unfamiliar to Roberta.

> ROBERTA
> Hey. Where we going?

> JOEL
> Just a little surprise.

> ROBERTA
> Food? I could definitely eat.

> JOEL
> Oh I suppose there'll be food there.

> ROBERTA
> Stop being so mysterious. Where are you taking me?

JOEL

I thought we'd pop by my brother's place and say hi.

ROBERTA

Your brother?

JOEL

You know. Tom. The one in the picture with the cute twins you're always gushing over.

ROBERTA
(All of a sudden not so sure)
He lives around here?

JOEL

Yeah. He and Cindy and the boys are probably just hanging out. They've got a great house.

ROBERTA

Don't you think maybe we should call first?

JOEL

Nahhh. They're always home. It's almost six. Maybe we can all order Chinese or something.

ROBERTA

Gee, Joel—you know maybe this isn't such a great idea?

JOEL

Oh don't worry. I always just drop in.

ROBERTA

No. I mean, could we visit them some other time?

JOEL
How come? We're almost there. It's like two minutes from here.

ROBERTA
Well my hair's a ball of knotted string and we stink of the beach and I don't have any clean clothes and—

JOEL
Don't worry, Roberta. We can shower there and you can borrow one of Cindy's shirts.

ROBERTA
(Firmly)
Joel. Honest. I'd really rather not. Can we please just go home?

Joel's Take:

"She doesn't want to meet my family, she hates me, the relationship is over!" That's the first thing Joel is going to think. Guys are very casual creatures. When we like you, we want to fit you into the family puzzle with no fuss or muss. But Joel should have realized that Roberta wouldn't want to meet everyone in cutoff shorts and a halter top. This is understandable.

FREE ADVICE: One, don't be surprised if you find yourself being introduced to a new boyfriend's family or friends at less than desirable times—like in bed! Or on a day when you're convinced that you look like you did your hair with a lawn mower! Two, if you must beg off, be very clear why, because you don't want him to think you're ducking the issue. Asking *you* to meet *them* is our way of making a very big statement: you're not just another girlfriend.

Home Improvements

The setup:

Richard and Mary have been dating for five months. Mary has been living with two roommates, and it's been difficult for Richard to spend nights with her because of roommate overload. When Mary gets a nice promotion and raise, she decides to move out and set up her first apartment on her own. Richard is ready and eager when moving day arrives. They've finished unloading the U-Haul, and now they're in her new digs, buried in boxes and mess. The situation is bleak.

> MARY
> (Overwhelmed and depressed)
> Where did all this stuff come from? I never dreamed I had so much junk.

> RICHARD
> Ahh yes. The flotsam and jetsam of life.

> MARY
> Yeah, and I need a cruise ship just to store it all.

> RICHARD
> No way. This is nothing.

> MARY
> That's easy for you to say. You have three hundred square feet more than me.

> RICHARD
> Now don't get blue. It's all in the organization. We just have to get some of these boxes out of here.

                    MARY

Sure. We'll throw out all my pots and pans.
My quilt collection. All my photo albums. My
stuffed animals. My computer and my stereo.
Then maybe we'll have room to fit my bed!

                   RICHARD

Nonsense. What we need to do is build some
great bookshelves.

                    MARY

Oh right. No sweat. The last time I tried to
hang a picture I broke my thumb trying to
nail up a hook.

                   RICHARD

Well you happen to be dating Mister Fixit.

                    MARY

Get out. You?

                   RICHARD
                (Feigning hurt)
Yes, me!

                    MARY

I'm sorry. I'm sure you're very handy. But I
don't think you can build a third room onto
an apartment building.

                   RICHARD

No, they may frown on that. But we can do
bookshelves on that whole north wall of the
living room. The kitchen needs some good
hanging hardware for your pots and pans.
And I think with a little planning we can
build a small loft space in your bedroom.

Maybe even raise the bed a couple of feet on a platform.

MARY

Hunghh?

RICHARD

You know. Raise it three feet and build a step up. Then I'll build you space drawers underneath for tons of your stuff.

MARY
(Cheering up)
Say, that's a great idea. But what about the bed being so high?

RICHARD
(Winking slyly)
It'll inspire us to new heights???

MARY

Oh really? Are you doing this for me or for you?

Richard's Take:

Clearly, he is doing it for himself. He's going to invest time and money and sweat and blood to make Mary's new home wonderful, because he's planning on spending a whole lot of time there. If Mary likes Richard, this is definitely to her advantage. While Richard wasn't ready to invite her to move into *his* place yet, his interest in her new space demonstrates that he can see notching the relationship up to the next level.

Career Crisis

The setup:

Danielle and Harry have been going out for a year. They like each other a lot, and there has even been talk of a real future together. They're out to dinner for a quick bite on a weekday night, and Danielle is in an absolutely dejected mood. She hasn't told Harry why, and he is working to get the goods out of her.

HARRY
You know you haven't said a word to me all night.

DANIELLE
What do you want me to say?

HARRY
Well, usually people who hang out together talk about something. You know, like the weather?

DANIELLE
It sucks. It's been raining for a week!

HARRY
(Scratching his chin)
Well, we're really communicating now.

DANIELLE
I'm sorry. I don't mean to be a jerk. It's just that, well—hmmmm.

HARRY
(Takes her hand)
Danielle! What's on your mind.

DANIELLE

Okay. It's about work.

HARRY

Tell me.

DANIELLE

Well the bad news is we lost several major advertising accounts this quarter, and they're going to downsize our office. Lots of people are going to lose their jobs.

HARRY

Are you one of them?

DANIELLE

That's sort of the bad news. I'm not.

HARRY

Am I missing something here? Why is that bad news?

DANIELLE

Well they really like me, and they want me to take a senior account exec position—

HARRY

That's great!

DANIELLE

In London.

Long pause.

HARRY

Oh.

DANIELLE

Exactly.

HARRY

And this is bad news?

DANIELLE

Not exactly. Not for my career.

HARRY

So what's the problem?

DANIELLE
(Gets angry at him)
Well what do you think the problem is?

HARRY
(Helplessly)
I give up.

DANIELLE

Oh, forget it.

HARRY

What did I do now?

DANIELLE

You're a guy. That's what you did. Like you'd
ever get it—

HARRY

Get what?

DANIELLE

Oh, maybe the four thousand miles between
you and me! Seeing each other twice a year, if
we're lucky. Phone sex until you find some
blond actress-type!

HARRY

I don't go for blondes.

DANIELLE

Very funny.

HARRY

So you're all upset because you have a great opportunity in London, and you're afraid that's going to separate us?

DANIELLE

It tends to put a damper on a relationship.

HARRY

And they don't have jobs for graphic artists in London?

DANIELLE

What are you saying?

HARRY

What do you think I'm saying?

DANIELLE

You mean if I had to move to London, you'd consider . . . I mean you might . . . you'd really think about coming with me?

Harry's Take:

"Yes!" Of course he would. If Danielle wanted him to. Guys have lots of ways of demonstrating their commitments. And for most men, there are certain steps they like to take before coughing up "the ring." Harry clearly cares for Danielle. They've been dating for a year. And she's considering an offer in London—not Siberia! A serious boyfriend would be thrilled to set off on an adventure like that with a woman he loves. It might be the step that leads them to move in together, or more. A man with good intentions will follow you around the globe, if you give him the opportunity.

Meeting Her Mom

The setup:

Maria and Glen have been seeing each other for several months and they're poised at the edge of getting serious. The one problem Maria has is that every time she wants to introduce Glen to her family, he balks. Once again they're together on a Saturday morning, and Maria is feeling pressure to bring Glen over to meet the family.

> MARIA
> Do we have any plans for tonight?

> GLEN
> Not that I know of. You want to see a movie or something?

> MARIA
> I don't know. We always go to the movies.

> GLEN
> You don't like movies?

> MARIA
> I love movies. But it'd be nice to do something else for a change.

> GLEN
> Wanna go to a ball game?

MARIA

No.

GLEN

Concert in the park?

MARIA

Not in the mood.

GLEN

Stay in and cook?

MARIA

We did that last night.

GLEN

Okay. I give up. What are we in the mood for tonight?

MARIA

Well, uhhh, can I ask you something?

GLEN

Anything.

MARIA

How come you refuse to meet my family?

GLEN

Hunghh?

MARIA

Every time I invite you over, you either have to work or you don't feel well or you start some huge project or—

GLEN

Wait one second. I don't recall—

MARIA
(Getting on a roll)
I hang out with all your friends. I do anything
you ask me to do.

GLEN
Maria, it's not that—

MARIA
We always do what *you* want to do. Why can't
we do something *I* want to do?

GLEN
(Shouts)
MARIA!

MARIA
(Pouting)
What?

GLEN
I was just thinking—why don't we do something with your family this weekend?

MARIA
(Truly surprised)
You really mean it?

GLEN
Is that what you want to do?

MARIA
We could just stop by for a drink. And then
we could go do whatever you want to do?
Would that be okay?

Glen's Take:

Just a drink? Why not Christmas dinner! After all this hoopla, you'd think Maria was trying to set up her own arranged marriage. We don't mind meeting your parents, especially if you don't make a big deal out of it. We're happy to be polite and say all the right things and meet anyone you like. It's the idea, more than anything, that scares most guys. If the meeting is staged like a scene from *The Godfather*, we tend to freak. If it's just a casual visit, we're incredibly more tolerant.

Boys at Play

The setup:

Marni and Stu have been dating for a year and they've recently moved in together. Of course with that upgrade in a relationship comes certain changes in the rules—two people new at cohabitation trying to allow one another some of the old freedoms. On this Saturday morning, Stu is packing for a week-long hiking trip with "the guys," and Marni is gamely lending a hand.

> MARNI
> It's going to be cold up there. Do you have enough sweaters?

> STU
> I think one and my windbreaker will be fine.

> MARNI
> Just don't want my honey freezing his cute buns off.

STU

My buns will be safely ensconced in my down sleeping bag.

MARNI

Missing my hot little hands I hope.

STU

Every second of the long, cold night.

MARNI

I think you should take more sweat socks. What if you get soaked? Two pairs may not dry.

STU

I'll be fine. And after four days I won't be needing them anyway.

MARNI

Of course you will. You guys are going for a week.

STU

No. *Those* guys are going for a week. I'm going until Wednesday!

MARNI

You're coming home early?

STU

No. I'm just not hiking for a week. Which sports coat should I take?

MARNI

Sports coat? What are you talking about, Stu?

STU
(Very nonchalant)
Oh, didn't I mention the fact that you're meeting me?

MARNI

Hunghh?

STU
Yeah. Your tickets are in my briefcase.

MARNI
Tickets for what?

STU

Montreal.

MARNI
Montreal?

STU
Yep. On Thursday morning. I'm hopping on a bus from the town where we're camping. I'll meet you at the hotel.

MARNI
What hotel? Stu—what are we doing?

STU
Well, I got to thinking a week with the guys might be a little much. And I'm going to miss you terribly—

MARNI
(Melting)
Stu—

STU

So, I thought you might like to meet me in old town Montreal next weekend. You don't mind, do you?

MARNI

But you've been looking forward to this trip for a year? I don't want you to miss time with your buddies.

STU

I've spent fifteen years hanging out with my buddies. You and I have lived together three months. You don't mind spending a little more time with me, do you?

MARNI

Will your friends ever talk to me again?

STU

Marni—my friends adore you. They love you. They all want to sleep with you!

MARNI
(Laughing)
I think I get the message.

STU

So are you up for Montreal?

MARNI

Wait 'til you see what I'm going bring! I promise you won't miss the guys. . . .

Stu's Take:

Any woman who cuts a man enough slack to take a week-long hiking trip with his buddies is worth her weight in gold. And along with that kind of freedom comes the classic male changeover. That would be the changeover from "one of the guys," to "one of the guys who has a girlfriend he loves."

FREE ADVICE: When you're first getting really involved with a man, or you move in together—don't be too harsh on his "buddy time." This is a big emotional change, and it might take a little while for him to adapt. A man will come around to enjoying all the quality time with you, when he realizes he still has a lot of freedom to see "the guys," and he doesn't have to cash it all in at once.

Love and Sex

The setup:

Tammy has been dating Paul for ten months. They spend all their weekends together, they see each other on week-nights, and they even have been known to sneak away in the middle of a workday afternoon, just because. Which happens to be the case on this day. They find themselves in bed, out of breath, spent from their stolen tryst.

PAUL
Tammy, what's wrong?

TAMMY
(Crying)
I don't know.

PAUL
Why are you crying?

                    TAMMY
Oh, it's nothing.

                    PAUL
It doesn't look like nothing. It looks like
something!

                    TAMMY
                (Sniveling)
No, I promise.

                    PAUL
Did I—we—do something bad just now?

                    TAMMY
No, it was great. Amazing!

She starts to cry again, even harder. Paul pulls her tight.

                    PAUL
Honey, honey. Just tell me. Are you—
                (Worried)
—tired of having sex with me?

                    TAMMY
                (Wiping her nose)
Of course not.

                    PAUL
Are you having an affair with another man?

                    TAMMY
Don't be ridiculous!

                    PAUL
                (Hopefully)
You're having an affair with another woman?

TAMMY

You wish.

PAUL
(Shrugging his shoulder)
Well—

TAMMY

I'm sorry. I didn't mean to get all emotional.
It's just when you called me at work and said
to race home? Just the way you sounded, and
looked—and made love to me—
(She starts crying again)
I'm sorry, Paul. . . .

PAUL

Sorry for *what?*

TAMMY
(Blurts it out)
Sorry because I love you so much. I've never
felt this way before. And when we were done
and I looked at you I got all scared like what
if I never see you again and I couldn't help
but start—

PAUL
(Wiping her tears)
Tammy, Tammy. It's okay.

TAMMY

It's not. It's silly. I'm acting like a sixteen-year-
old.

PAUL

It's not silly. You're acting like—you.

TAMMY

And that's silly.

PAUL

And I think it's wonderful.

TAMMY
(Meekly)

You do?

PAUL

Yes, as a matter of fact I do.

TAMMY

Honest?

PAUL

Honest.

TAMMY

So you don't hate me? You're not going to leave me.

PAUL

Tammy, you could cry every single time we made love, and I'd only love you more. . . .

Paul's Take:

There comes a time in every man's life when sex evolves into love. That usually happens on the day we realize we're with a woman we could spend the rest of our lives with. It has nothing to do with the quality of the sex and everything to do with the honesty of your emotions. Men are not trained to cry. Only to *respond* to tears. A woman who cries during lovemaking is sending a message, and if you're with the right guy, he will be all too happy to receive it.

The Moment of Truth

The setup:

Lisa and John are celebrating the anniversary of their first date by spending the weekend in Vermont. They've been hiking all day and as the sun begins to set, they find themselves sitting on a hill above a meadow, looking out over the mountains. They are alone, and it is very quiet. There is nothing but the sound of the breeze over a hayfield.

LISA
(Her arm around John)
What are you thinking about, honey?

JOHN
(Thoughtfully)
Nothing.

LISA
You seem so quiet.

JOHN
Hmmm. I guess I am.

LISA
It's pretty up here.

JOHN
Sure is.

They sit in silence a little longer.

> LISA
> Are you sure you're okay?

> JOHN
> Promise.

> LISA
> I'm glad. . . . I'm really happy, you know.

> JOHN
> Really?

> LISA
> Yeah. I mean happy up here and with you and, well, just with everything.

> JOHN
> (After a long pause)
> You know, I am, too.

> LISA
> Are you?

> JOHN
> Happier than I've ever been in my life.

> LISA
> You're giving me goose bumps. . . .

They sit silently and watch the sun going down over the mountains.

> JOHN
> (Taking a deep breath)
> Lisa?

LISA

Yeah?

JOHN

I've been thinking, and, uhhh . . . I, uhhh, I—
(Another deep breath)
Would you spend your life with me?

LISA
(Eyes welling up)

John—

JOHN

I mean, would you like to marry me?

LISA

Yes. Yes!

JOHN

Yes, you'd like to spend your life with me?

LISA
(Beaming through her tears)

Yes, I'd like to spend my life with you.
Yes, I'd like to marry you. . . .

They look at each other and hug, then kiss, and then look
at each other again.

JOHN
(Seriously)

Lisa?

LISA

What?

JOHN
(After a long pause)
What do we do now?

LISA
(Laughing and crying)
Whatever it was we were doing before . . .

John's Take:

Why does a man finally ask a woman to marry him? Because after all the years of flirting and dating and fooling around and trying to figure the whole thing out—he suddenly just knows! Some guys may be the "engagement ring in the ice cube type," and others may be the "spur of the moment sunset proposal" type. But either way, the moment of truth hits a man because the woman he's with makes his heart and mind do flip-flops at all the right times.

FREE ADVICE: If you're dating a man and you know he's the one? Just take love, laughter, and passion—add patience, compassion, and understanding—and the rest is sure to follow.